Disorder

Legal Laughs, Court Jests and Just Jokes Culled From the Nation's Justice System

WITH A FOREWORD BY RICHARD LEDERER

Library of Congress Catalog Card Number: 96-067522
ISBN 1-881859-11-8
Copyright 1996, National Court Reporters Association
8224 Old Courthouse Road
Vienna, VA 22182

Foreword

Hear ye! Hear ye! Court will now come to disorder!

Most language is spoken language, and most words, once they are uttered, vanish forever into the air. But such is not the case with language spoken during courtroom trials, for there exists an army of court reporters whose job it is to take down and preserve every statement made during these proceedings. Recording in shorthand every syllable uttered during hearings, depositions, trials and sentencings, America's court reporters are literally America's keepers of the word.

That is the special appeal of courtroom bloopers. We know that the uncut gems gleaming out from transcripts are authentic, genuine, certified and uncut. We know that they are not manufactured and polished by some professional humorist. That's because, for decades, court reporters have snared and then shared their favorite court jests, which they call "transquips." Transquips are woven from whole cloth, with a bit of lunatic fringe. Only real life itself could produce

this courtroom classic:

Q. What is your brother-in-law's name?
A. Borofkin.
Q. What is his first name?
A. I can't remember.
Q. He's been your brother-in-law for 45 years, and you can't remember his first name?
A. No, I tell you I'm too excited. (Rising from the witness chair and pointing to Mr. Borofkin) Nathan, for God's sake, tell them your first name!

Another reason that transquips detonate the reader's stomach into a rolling boil is their unique mix of seriousness and humor. It is ironic the regularity with which laughter invades that most hallowed of all venues, the legal inner sanctum. H.L. Mencken once observed, "The penalty for laughing in a courtroom is six months; if it were not for this penalty, the jury would never hear the evidence." Transquips are the cracked side of the gripping trial scenes we see in movies and read about in novels. In real-life courtrooms, lawyers can ask the weirdest questions, witnesses can say the darnedest things and high drama often turns into low comedy.

You wouldn't believe some of the things that tumble out of lawyers' mouths in the heat of battle or the throes of boredom. All attorneys have those days when they think their brains belong to Daniel Webster and Clarence Darrow but their tongues belong to Elmer Fudd and Daffy Duck.

Q. How many times have you committed suicide?

Q. You were there until the time you left, is that true?

Running the mouth before putting the brain in gear also afflicts many a witness:

DEFENDANT: I can't pay the fine because I'm disabled.
JUDGE: What's your problem?
DEFENDANT: All my glands is prostrated.

Q. James stood back and shot Tommy Lee?
A. Yes.
Q. And then Tommy Lee pulled out the gun and shot James in the fracas?
A. (After a hesitation) No sir, just above it.

Fortunately for all of us, Mary Louise Gilman, longtime editor of the *National Shorthand Reporter*, bloopthologized many of the best transquips in *Humor in the Court* (1977) and *More Humor in the Court* (1984). And, in fact, she also had a hand in this book, which contains the best transquips of the past dozen years. To her, who defined the genre of courtroom blunders, this book is justly dedicated.

Life is a little brighter because a troop of court reporters has been stationed in our halls of justice to capture all the gavel to gabble laughter. Each of the examples of disorder in the court you are about to read is on public record, all taken down by America's keepers of the word. May their tribe increase and multiply.

Richard Lederer
Author of *Anguished English*

Table of Contents

Comedians in the Court

Paying for It

Q. So you got the opinions of two lawyers on your case. Were they the same?

A. Yes, $25 each.

Parting Shot

MR. FANTA: I have no further questions of this obviously incompetent witness.

THE WITNESS: Did you say "incontinent" or "incompetent"?

MR. FANTA: Both. You are just pissing in the wind anyway.

A Case of Nerves

Q. Were you in any kind of pain?

A. It wasn't pain that hurt. It was just such an annoyance being not able to hear. I was just afraid I was losing my ear sight. My ear sight?

Q. Hearing?

A. Ear sight, eye sight. You can't tell I'm nervous, can you?

2

Unanimity

JUDGE: Well, gentlemen of the jury, are you unanimous?

FOREMAN: Yes, your Honor, we're all alike — temporarily insane.

Wrong Jurisdiction

FEDERAL JUDGE: This seems like a fairly simple problem. Let's not make a federal case out of it.

Great Play on Words, But ...

THE COURT: Do you have a license yet?

THE DEFENDANT: No, sir, I don't. I have a judgement against me. I don't have a car either.

THE COURT: Well, it didn't stop you before, did it?

THE DEFENDANT: No, but—

THE COURT: But? No buts. We just look at the facts cold without dressing them up. If you have the but there you're trying to put a dress on it. Look at it in its natural state.

Which Leg?
Q. Do you have any other complaints?

A. Even my sex life, I think, has been affected.

Q. How has it been affected?

A. Because one of my legs is no good.

A Direct Response
Q. Do you recall approximately the time that you examined the body of Mr. Edgington at the Rose Chapel?

A. It was in the evening. The autopsy started about 8:30 p.m.

Q. And Mr. Edgington was dead at that time, is that correct?

A. No, you dumb asshole. He was sitting there on the table wondering why I was doing an autopsy.

Process of Elimination

Q. Was he short or tall or fat or skinny?

A. I think he was tall. He was taller than me.

Q. You were nine years old?

MR. MORRIS: We have eliminated the fact that he was a dwarf.

Case in Point

Q. I have a few questions I'd like to ask you. I'll ask that you respond in such a manner that I can hear your answer. Fair enough?

A. (Witness nodded head.)

Q. I didn't hear that answer.

I Try to Be Nice

Q. Well, sir, judging from your answer on how you reacted to the emergency call, it sounds like you are a man of intelligence and good judgment.

A. Thank you, and if I weren't under oath I'd return the compliment.

Not Again!

Q. Those are all the questions I have. Did you understand the questions that you answered?

A. Most of them, yes.

Q. Are there any that you think you didn't understand?

A. There was a few of them that I wasn't sure — well, no, I don't guess.

Q. What areas are there that you think you weren't clear on?

A. Can you go back through the questions again?

A Problem With What?

Q. Do you consider yourself to have a good memory?

A. Over short periods of time.

Q. Has anyone ever told you that you have a problem with your memory?

A. Not that I remember.

It's a Fair Assumption

Q. And you are assuming that she's going to live beyond the year 62, until under some actuarial tables that statistically she would die; is that right?

A. Yes, I'm assuming she would live until she dies.

How to Lose Five Trucks — Instantly

Q. How many trucks do you own?

A. Seventeen.

Q. Seventy?

A. Seventeen.

Q. Seventeen?

A. No, about 12.

Witness Goulash

Q. So what you're telling me today, and today is January 27, 1987, about what occurred in July of 1982 is more accurate than what you said on December 4, 1985?

A. Absolutely. It's more accurate because I was not working there then until I had went back.

Q. OK. Do you understand the meaning of an oath?

A. What's an oath?

Matters of Life and Death

Q. Did your wife's illness become somewhat progressively worse between 1979 and 1986?

A. She died. It had to get somewhat worse.

They Just Helped Him Along

Q. And what were the circumstances where you were set up to do that?

A. There was a case here in Salinas in which two ladies of the night drowned their—

Q. Customer?

A. —customer in a tub, and attempted to steal his money and leave town. They were apprehended, and the defense was that he had a bad heart, and would have died anyway. And the District Attorney thought there was probably some more to it than that.

Just Call

A. I can remember my father-in-law calling me one time and saying that Estelle was disoriented.

Q. That was prior to his death?

A. Well, it had to be, if he called me.

Q. So, that was prior—

A. Or it was a mighty long-distance call.

Buckle Up, James

Q. Miss Ball, do you know whether in fact James put his seat belt on, or are you just surmising he didn't?

A. I know that he didn't put his seat belt on.

Q. What is your personal observation of that?

A. Because when we were driving down the street James was mooning people through the back window.

Q. Kind of hard to moon people with a seat belt on?

A. That's right.

There's Gold in Them Thar Transcripts

Q. Do you know Mr. John Smith?

A. Yes.

Q. Do you know how I can get in touch with him?

A. Yes, I have his number at home.

Q. Do you know Jane Johnson?

A. Yes.

Q. Do you know how I can get in touch with her?

A. I think I have her number at home.

Q. Do you know David Smith?

A. Yes, he's dead.

Q. Do you know how I can get in touch with him — well, no, I guess you wouldn't.

A. No, I don't have those kinds of connections.

Hard to Say

Q. My question is, do you suffer from any specifically diagnosed medical condition like Alzheimer's disease or anything that would specifically contribute to the hampering of your memory?

A. Not that I remember.

The Stud

Q. The bull was an effort to try to get your breeding improved?

A. Yes.

Q. And did that work totally?

A. No. It helped, but when the vet came for herd health, going through the herd and pregnancy checking, he would go through the cows ... and he says, well, looks like Roy didn't get her this time.

MR. JONES: Objection, hearsay.

THE COURT: Sustained.

Q. What did they tell you in this case, Roy didn't get her?

A. Yeah, that was the name of the bull.

THE COURT: Glad it wasn't the hired man.

Fair Warning

Q. Who's your supervisor over there?

A. They call him Animal. I don't know his last name.

Q. Just Animal?

MR. PETERS: You might want to warn the process server.

Picture This

THE COURT: When the officers came on the scene, and they were called there for a reason, and you were completely out of control. No question in my mind. You were salivating. The testimony was that — just picture in your own mind what you must have looked like salivating.

A. Kind of like Old Yeller before they shot him, I guess.

Judicial Honesty

MR. SMITH: If it please the Court, I'm the person who drew the findings. They're slightly at variance with the decision, but I think they're based upon some common sense and also some circumstances that have changed since the Court gave its oral decision.

THE COURT: It has happened that judicial decisions are at variance with common sense.

Who's to Blame?

Q. Do you understand my question?

A. I think so, but that may be my fault.

I Cannot Tell a Lie — Really!

From a sentencing hearing where the Court had ordered the "drug dog" to search the defendant's residence:

THE COURT: Well, should we arrange to get the dog over there? How does that sound to you, Mr. Killion?

THE DEFENDANT: I could give it to you, sir.

THE COURT: The problem is, I don't believe you. I don't believe you would admit anything that you weren't absolutely certain would be proven.

THE DEFENDANT: Please, trust me.

THE COURT: Why? You are a convicted felon and a compulsive liar.

THE DEFENDANT: With the Lord being on my side, I—

THE COURT: I figured we'd get to that in a moment. I suppose if the Lord is really on your side, the dog would come down with a head cold.

New Wave Music, No Doubt

THE COURT: Could you run through that list of stuff again? The mixer, microwave, et cetera.

WIFE'S COUNSEL: It is a VCR, a CD player, a mixer, walkie-talkie, microwave, tape player, half of the CDs and tapes, and the cables which attach to those items.

THE COURT: Is the microwave and mixer on there?

WIFE'S COUNSEL: No, the mixer would have to do with the stereo system, not the typical kitchen mixer.

THE COURT: Was there a microwave?

WIFE'S COUNSEL: There was a microwave.

THE COURT: That's not the name of an album, is it?

Older?

Q. You said something that made me think he was a pretty young guy.

A. He was an older gentleman. He's, I guess, would be late 30s.

Having a High Opinion

    Q. How would you describe yourself—

    A. A hell of a nice guy.

    Q. —if you were to describe your duties—

Who Do You Love?

    Q. Tell us your full name, please.

    A. Mine?

    Q. Yes, sir.

    A. 555-2723.

    Q. Mr. Daniels, do you have any problems hearing me?

    A. Not really.

    Q. Where do you live?

    A. Pardon?

In the Eyes of the Beholder

Q. Can you tell the Court what that man looked like?

A. He's kind of an Oriental guy, Puerto Rican, sort of Oriental.

Q. When you mentioned Oriental, you mean like Chinese or Japanese?

A. No, Arab. Something like that.

Q. What does an Arab look like?

A. To me?

Q. Yes.

A. Like a Mexican.

A Difficult Deposition

Q. The rules of perjury provide that if you lie to us today, it's a serious offense which carries prison time.

A. He's asking me about all my person life to tell the truth in about all my life or only about this case, my case?

Q. I'm sorry. Were you under the impression that you were only supposed to tell the truth with respect to the case?

A. That's a loaded question.

Timing Is Everything

Q. When did he scratch his initials into the watch?

A. I couldn't tell you, but it was previous to his death.

That Bites

Q. Did you see anything else there in relation to the gun, or just the gun and two rounds?

A. And a dog.

Q. And a dog, right.

THE COURT: Anything unusual about the dog?

THE WITNESS: Yes. He bit it.

The Experts' Expert

Q. Now, Mr. Johnson, are you trained to determine which way water flows?

A. Yes. That's something that can be determined by the surveying process.

Q. How do you determine the direction in which water flows?

A. Well, water flows downhill.

A Matter of Direction

Q. I have never been at that apartment complex so I will ask you if you can describe for me, when you came out of your apartment on the second floor, where was the elevator in relation to your apartment?

A. Where was the elevator? I don't know where the elevator was. It would be up or down.

Some Deponents Are Like That

Q. And why did you leave college?

A. They caught me on the third floor of the girls' dorm and decided they didn't want me back.

Q. I see. So you had some sort of a rules violation at college?

A. I believe that's putting it lightly.

(A little later, in the same deposition:)

Q. Are there any activities that cause you problems or any limitations with your leg that you have noticed?

A. Well, I can't keep time to the music as good with my right leg as I can with my left.

(And a final exchange involving the deponent, who had fallen off a roof and injured himself:)

Q. Can you tell me just how you were injured?

A. Sure. I hit the ground hard.

Q. Well, did you take a flying leap, or did you fall off a ladder, or how did it happen?

A. Oh, I had this planned for years. Turkey!

Q. I'm just wondering.

A. I stepped onto the parapet wall, and my foot went out from under me, and I headed for a sudden stop.

Q. How far do you suppose you fell?

A. Twenty-two feet, nine inches. I don't know how far I fell!

Q. Far enough to injure yourself, apparently?

A. Yeah. And that concrete ain't very damn forgiving, either.

Here, Take My Hamsters!

Q. When was the most recent time Timmy cried over this incident?

A. When we were served with our own personal lawsuit.

Q. Did he tell you why he was crying?

A. Yes.

Q. What did he say?

A. He was afraid he was going to lose his hamsters and his bedroom.

Q. Did he tell you why he felt that?

A. Because he didn't know what a lawsuit was.

Q. Did you assure him that nobody was going to be taking his hamsters?

A. I assured him no one was going to take his hamsters. I wasn't sure about the bedroom.

The Gods Help Those ...

Q. I take it you helped milk the cows?

A. I milked them.

Q. Did you help with breeding at all?

A. In regard to what? The bulls did the breeding. I couldn't do that.

Q. You've got me there.

Small Restriction

Q. Are you restricted in some way by having your third finger shot off?

A. Yeah, a little.

Q. What could you do before the accident that you can't do now?

A. Wear a ring on it.

Could Be Worse

Q. Now, Mr. Kowalski, you realize you have been placed under oath this afternoon?

A. Yes, I do.

Q. And what does that mean to you?

A. Tell the truth.

Q. If you don't tell the truth, what could happen to you?

A. Go to hell.

Q. Or something worse, go to the Marinette County Jail.

A. Yeah.

You Just Had to Say it, Didn't You?

Q. In other words, beyond the nonreimbursability, there is no other fine imposed, they're just not reimbursed?

A. There could be at the claim committee level.

Q. But just so we are clear on this, let's keep "fine" separate from "nonreimbursability"?

A. Fine.

Anyone for Lunch?

MR. OSTENSON: Could you go back and find a place in the record where I first asked the witness about Samaritan Health Service's intentions with regard to trying to keep Mayo out of Scottsdale?

THE COURT REPORTER: Question: "Did Mr. Teng say that he had agreed with Mayo that Mayo would not build a tertiary-care hospital in the Scottsdale area?"

Answer: "No. I think I would have remembered that."

Question: "Did Mr. Teng say that he had discussed SHS's desire not to have the Mayo Clinic build a tertiary-care hospital in the Scottsdale area?"

Q. So what Mr. Teng said was, "Hold the Mayo?"

We Just Say "Hey, You"

Q. How did you get here today?
A. I had a friend bring me.
Q. The friend's name?
A. We call him Fifi.
Q. To his face?

The Worm Turns

Q. Which federal prison was that?

A. It was at Terre Haute, Indiana.

Q. Excuse me?

A. Terre Haute, Indiana.

Q. You need not shout, Mr. O'Brien.

A. I was being articulate.

Q. Well, I'm sorry if I'm being redundant, but that's my job.

A. And you do it very well.

I Can Say It

Q. The hospital is to the right?

A. It was on this side.

Q. When you say this side, can you say right or left?

A. Yeah, right or left.

Open Mouth, Insert Foot

Q. Humerus is what? What is the right humerus? It is a bone?

A. The right humerus is the humerus that is on the opposite side of the body of the left humerus.

I'll Bring the Chips

Q. Was there a specific occasion for your discarding that file?

A. I don't understand the question. What do you mean, "specific occasion"? Did I throw a party?

Going to Extremes

A. So when she came back that summer to the dormitory she basically wanted to put that reputation behind her.

Q. What reputation?

A. The reputation of being a casual drug user.

Q. She wanted to put that behind her and become a full-fledged drug user?

Professional Courtesy

Q. Are you familiar with the Manual of Uniform Traffic Control Devices?

A. Yes, I am.

Q. What does that manual say about trimming trees around a stop sign?

A. I don't know, quite honestly. As I understand it, at least five times as many attorneys purchase that manual as traffic engineers, so you would be more familiar with it than I am.

Duty Roster

Q. Is that general maintenance personnel that you referred to?

A. Do you want actual numbers?

Q. If you can recall.

A. Nine preventive mechanics, one general maintenance, a support services manager, three groundskeepers, four decorators, one lead decorator, three carpenters, two electricians, two plumbers, one parts coordinator and one refrigeration mechanic.

MR. LEMIRE: And a partridge in a pear tree.

A Smoking Gun

A. It was a tight chest, having a hard time catching air.

Q. And did this come on suddenly?

A. Yeah. It was the first time I experienced it.

Q. Where were you when it came on?

A. In bed.

Q. Sleeping, or were you—

A. You really want to know?

Q. I just want to know if it was activity induced.

A. I was having sex.

Q. I think we could say it was activity induced. And had you had a cigarette any time around this time?

A. No, of course I was not smoking during sex. My wife asked me once, "Do you smoke after sex?" I said, "I've never looked down there to see."

MS. WALLACE: You asked.

A Smart Aleck

Q. And do you see your dad in court?

A. Not often.

Be Careful What You Ask

Q. And where was the location of the accident?

A. Approximately milepost 499.

Q. And where is milepost 499?

MR. SMITH: Probably between milepost 498 and milepost 500.

He Just Couldn't Resist

Q. You mentioned, sir, that you have been stung by a scorpion?

A. Yeah.

Q. When was that, do you recall?

A. Let's see. We'll say '80.

Q. And what part of your body was stung?

A. My hand.

Q. And what steps did you take after you were stung?

A. Oh, about three.

Q. All right. I asked for that.

A. I couldn't help it. I had to throw that one in there.

Aggrieved Witness

Q. Was Mr. French present on the day of this incident of the confrontation that happened between you and Mr. Brewer?

A. Yes, he was in the office when Mr. Brewer walked back and came directly to me. He caught me off guard because it was surprising. And before I realized it, I made some remarks that are regrettable. But it was done under — he aggrieved me with malice aforethought and intimidating litigations, and I just reacted.

Dr. Comedian

Q. How did you find her on that date?

A. Opened the exam room door, there she was.

Tongue Twisters and Mental Somersaults

"Can I help it if my only witness was the guy I killed?"

The Long and Short of It

MR. RAYES: Your Honor, I have a short witness, and Mr. Dyer has agreed to take him out of order.

THE COURT: How short?

MR. RAYES: It is Mr. Long.

THE COURT: No problem with interrupting?

MR. DYER: Not at all, your Honor.

THE COURT: Put Long on.

MR. DYER: As long as he is short.

Relevance

MR. SLACK: OK, I will cross-examine not because it is relevant, but I want to ask an additional question of this witness that I also feel is irrelevant but relevant to what is irrelevant.

Crystal Clear

Q. What did he say that you said you're now saying you didn't say?

A. You say what? Some of the things I said or he said that I said, right?

Q. Right.

A. Aren't true.

Q. But you did tell him those things?

A. Right.

Hearing Problems

Q. When you said that, there was some hesitation. Have you heard of others that you haven't heard about yet?

I Ask You

MR. BENJAMIN: I will object as vague and ambiguous, calls for speculation.

You can answer, if you understand the question.

THE WITNESS: Well, I understand that he's asking me what I think he's asking me.

MR. BENJAMIN: What do you think he's asking you?

THE WITNESS: I think he's asking me what I think he means. I think I can tell him what I think he means. Whether or not it's what he means is another story.

Eternal Job-Hunter

Q. Can you give us your business background, starting with the first job you held?

A. It's rather numerous.

Q. We'll wait.

A. I don't remember if I had many jobs.

Q. I'm sorry?

A. I don't remember if I had many jobs.

Q. You don't remember if you had many jobs, or any jobs?

A. Either or.

Pinning it Down

Q. And when was that?

A. I guess it was sometime before noon or after noon.

Redundant Response

Q. Do you know how many occasions you have had contact with Ms. Washington?

A. Prior to this day, I would say six times, maybe half a dozen at the very most.

I Went There to Buy a Geography Book

Q. I notice from the rehabilitation reports that you were recently in Mexico; is that correct?

A. They lied. I did not go to Mexico. I went to Tijuana.

A Common Problem

A. I really cannot answer this question because I'm not sure, and I'm not sure what I'm talking about.

Been Forging My Paycheck?

Q. Have you ever been convicted of a crime?

A. Yes.

Q. And what was that crime?

A. It was for an insignificant funds check.

Say What?

Q. Can you give me a single reason why you wouldn't have told Daniel that you believed the product was well designed?

A. The fact that I might have no reason not to say something doesn't mean I said it, and I don't — I don't see what that has to do that I might not have a reason to say it and the inference that I did say it because I had no reason not to.

Know Jimmy Jones Well

Q. Do you know the defendant?

A. Yes.

Q. Did you see the defendant shoot these people?

A. No. I seen it was Jimmy Jones.

Q. Do you know Jimmy Jones?

A. Yes, I know Jimmy Jones very well.

Q. And this man who you saw shoot these people, could you tell if he was white or black?

A. I don't know if he was white or black, but I know it was Jimmy Jones because I know Jimmy Jones.

Mechanical Poetry

Q. Anything else you found that had to be repaired?

A. Specifications stipulated ring tape gaskets at raised face flanges and full face gaskets at flat face flanges.

Say Again

Q. Where is Gary Horowitz?

A. Corpus Christi.

Q. Is he a friend or a bookie?

A. Mostly a bookie.

Q. Who else?

A. Clyde Dodd.

Q. Dodd?

A. Yeah, he's dead.

Q. Dead?

A. He's very dead.

MR. CLAPP: He died, Dodd?

A. Clyde died.

Q. In degrees of death, he's at the extreme?

A. Yes.

Tedious Testimony

Q. So I am correct when I say that you haven't discussed your testimony that you are giving here today with anybody?

A. No.

MR. TABLER: That's not correct.

THE WITNESS: Today.

MR. TABLER: No, he's not asking you if you just talked to somebody today about your testimony today, whether you talked to anybody about your testimony today on any day.

THE WITNESS: Yes.

MR. TABLER: That's what I thought.

Assumptions

Q. Did he tell you that he had himself assumed that loan?

A. Yes, he did.

Q. That was on the basis of that he said it was assumable?

A. I don't know what basis he said that he assumed it and it was assumable. He didn't say that he assumed it was assumable because he assumed it.

Let Me Rephrase That

Q. Since the time — well, let me put it this way. Nowadays, do you ever have trouble getting an erection?

A. It's — it's harder than before.

MR. JONES: You mean harder to get one?

THE WITNESS: No — right, it's hard to get.

MR. JONES: It's more difficult?

THE WITNESS: Yes.

MR. SMITH: Off the record.

Not That I Remember

Q. You have no recollection of doing that?

A. I was trying to remember if there was anything I couldn't have remembered, but I doubt very much if there was anything I even forgot.

Distinction Without a Difference

Q. So you don't recall the exact distance?

A. That he was from me? Or I was from him?

He Knows What He Knows

Q. What do you think he knows?

A. I think Larry knows the truth.

Q. And which is?

A. You mean as far as the job was concerned?

Q. You said he knows the truth. What is the truth?

A. Concerning what?

Q. What Larry knows.

A. I think he knows everything about it.

We Trust it Wasn't a Weapons Charge

MR. MARSHALL: Your Honor, with respect to sentencing, it's Mr. Watkins' request that his surrender date be delayed until after October 1. He's already purchased his hunting license. It's basically nonrefundable, and he'd like to at least get half the deer season in before he has to surrender himself.

THE COURT: Let's keep things in proper perspective. Let's go to the end of hunting season, if need be. Take care of the important things in life.

Mop Flop

Q. Were you ever in the service?

A. Yes.

Q. What branch?

A. Navy.

Q. Did you get an honorable discharge?

A. No.

Q. Was it dishonorable?

A. No.

Q. What was it?

A. I don't know.

Q. What did it say on the discharge?

A. Unable to mop.

Postal Carrier Develops Hernia

Q. Did you notify Mr. Davis you wanted him to return the cab?

A. Yes. I sent him a letter to return the cab by registered mail.

I Don't Know

Q. Did you dispose of them or throw them away?
A. I don't know. I did not, no.
Q. Did you give them to anyone else?
A. I did not, no.
Q. Who knows?
A. I said, I did not.
Q. Oh, you did not?
A. I did not.
Q. Who would know?
A. I don't know.

Had You Worried, Huh?

THE COURT: Defendant is remanded to the custody of the Sheriff, who is ordered to carry into execution the order of the Court.

THE DEFENDANT: Judge, can I say something?

THE COURT: Sure.

THE DEFENDANT: Did you say, "Executed"?

THE COURT: No. You got 30 years, Mr. Ashford.

The Smell of the Courtroom

Q. Why was Mr. Stenger suspended?

A. Because Mr. Stenger stunk.

Q. Why did Mr. Stenger stink?

A. He didn't have fresh overalls.

Q. Because he didn't have fresh overalls, Mr. Stenger stunk?

A. I don't recall that he said Mr. Stenger stunk. He was sitting next to him and said he did stink.

Q. Did you ever confirm with other employees whether Mr. Stenger stunk?

A. To my recollection nobody indicated that he stunk.

Q. Did you believe Mr. Stenger had a hygiene problem?

A. Do you mean did he stink? Yes, Mr. Stenger stunk.

Series of Events

Q. Did you stop along the way?

A. Several times. We stopped several times because of the little boy. And we ate at least twice that I know of, and we got gas.

Sound Clarification

Q. I believe that you testified you met him on one occasion?

A. That's correct, when we formally spoke.

Q. And the total of your conversation with him was an introduction and a "hi"?

A. Not even an introduction, just a "hi."

MR. SMITH: Excuse me. In light of the public history, do you want to spell "hi" for me, please? Is that h-i?

THE WITNESS: H-i. It wasn't a question, it was just a greeting.

Seems a Bit Extreme

THE COURT: Do you have a motion to make at this time?

MR. MELLMAN: Yes. At this time, your Honor, we would move that the jury be discharged and the jury be hung because of inability to reach a verdict.

Normal Confusion
Q. Did you return to Normal after the phone call?
MR. ANDERSON: Normal, Illinois, I take it?

Water Cooler Gossip
A. He kept everybody in their — kind of — I was under him just specifically to do certain things. And really nobody in the office really knows what I was doing.

Looking Out for Number One
Q. Would it be at or about the time of this letter to Mr. Stephenson in June of '84 or did you know about him before that time?
A. I don't recall. I, number one, was gone and I thought you meant Mr. Stephenson there for a minute. Oh, I meant number one, I — no, not number one — number one, just number one.

Reasonably Good Communication

THE WITNESS: First of all, there is another whole set of problems which we would have constructive notice of that he wouldn't have to, quote, unquote, "bring to our particular attention," just because he would know we knew, and we would know he knew we knew and therefore we would have notice. We were in reasonably good communication with the contractor.

Thank God Someone Does

Q. Well, I just want it understood that what I'm asking is whether or not you understood whether or not it was going to happen, or whether or not it was true you understood.

A. I understand.

Yes or No

Q. Can you answer that yes or no?

A. Can I answer? I don't think it is my place to answer it yes or no.

Q. Can you answer it?

A. Yes or no?

Q. That is your answer, yes or no?

A. No, my question to you.

Q. You don't ask the question.

THE COURT: Can you answer his question?

A. Can you repeat the question?

(The reporter read the requested question.)

A. I don't believe I can answer that yes or no.

Clear-as-Mud Dept.

Q. We've talked about a number of drafts now. Is that the final draft that was issued sometime in January?

A. This is the final revised revision of the revised revision revised.

For Four?

Q. So your license was suspended for years before this accident?

A. Yes.

MR. DALE: Let me object to that. I don't think it was four years.

MS. DOYLE: It's f-o-r.

MR. DALE: I don't think it was four years.

MS. DOYLE: No, not four years.

MR. DALE: No, I don't think it was suspended for four years. I think it was suspended for years before the accident, not four years.

MS. DOYLE: Yes. That's what I understood the testimony to be.

MR. DALE: OK.

Getting it Right

Q. What does 3-16 show?

A. It's a plan view of the driver's side of the vehicle.

Q. Did you say planned, p-l-a-n-n-e-d?

A. No; p-l-a-n. That means a top view.

Q. Oh. A plane view?

A. Plan is a top view.

Q. Planned view?

A. No, no. Not planned; p-l-a-n, plan view.

Q. Oh, p-l-a-n, plan view.

A. If you're looking at a set of plans, it's from the top.

Q. Understood. I just wanted to make sure we had the right word on the record.

Joe Bob

Q. So you were relating to Joe what Bob told you Joe said to Bob?

A. And when I confronted Joe and he admitted to.

Confusing Clarification

    Q. Is that what you wrote?

    A. That's what I wrote.

    Q. That's incorrect; is that correct?

    A. That's not incorrect.

    Q. That's correct?

    A. That's correct.

Concerning Concerns

    Q. Do you recall whether you had discussions about your concerns?

    A. Did I discuss these concerns, or did I discuss my concern about the concern that I would be fired if I objected too much?

    Q. I guess your concerns about raising these concerns. Whether you ever discussed that you were concerned about raising these concerns, if you were so concerned.

Who Knows Dept.

A. You know, I don't know, but I mean, you know — you don't know but you know. You know what I'm saying?

Q. No, I'm not quite sure I know what you mean by that.

A. A lot of times a person may think they know, but when they think about it they realize that they don't know. It is not that we want to know what you don't know, but we want to know that you don't know, and we want to know what you know. Do you know what I mean?

Q. Do I? No. Do I know? No.

As You Well Know

MR. BERNS: You can have a continuing objection, but I'm sure, as you well know, it is the law in the state that any specialist who is relying on the report of another specialist who is the type of specialist upon whom the first specialist customarily relies is entitled to so rely and is entitled to so address the diagnoses with which he is provided by the referred specialist.

"Who's On First?" Dept.

Q. Is there a device that is manufactured by Wood something or other or Moore something or other?

A. It is a signal that is seen by a Moore something or other.

MR. ZAPPA: What are we talking about here? You have lost me.

MR. BUXTON: I don't know; I am trying to find out.

MR. ZAPPA: Well, make sure you understand. When we get into something or others, it gets confusing.

Q. What is it?

A. What is what?

Q. Moore something or other?

A. That is doing what?

Q. What he said.

A. No.

MR. BUXTON: Would you read back where he said something signals something.

Holding it in Escrow

Q. What did you do with the money?

A. My attorney told me to put it in escrow.

Q. And did you do that?

A. Yes, sir.

Q. And where is that account located?

A. I told you, in escrow.

Q. Yes, but where is it being held, in what financial institution?

A. I can't remember the name of the bank, but I know it's in escrow.

Q. Do you know the city or the state where it is being held?

A. It's in Escrow, Ohio.

Q. Where is that?

A. I don't know, but if you have a map, we can probably find it.

A Simple Name

Q. Do you remember who the doctor was who performed that?

A. Yes. Very easy name to remember, Mee.

Q. Martin? (The witness's name.)

A. No, Mee.

Q. You?

A. That was his name.

Q. Me?

A. Mee.

Q. M-e?

A. M-e-e. That was his name, Dr. Mee.

Let's Beat a Dead Horse While We're at It

Q. That happened occasionally?

A. Yeah, very occasionally.

Q. Very infrequently?

A. No.

Q. Yes, it was frequent?

A. It wasn't infrequently.

Q. It wasn't frequent?

A. No.

Q. Infrequently, in other words, not frequent.

A. Infrequent.

Is Everyone Clear Now?

Q. What are the locations of the places where you have been arrested as Joseph Carone?

A. One time I remembered it was in a warehouse in Chinatown that's called Ching Gow Garden.

THE WITNESS: (In English) Greenfield Far. Greenfield Farm.

THE INTERPRETER: Greenfield—

THE WITNESS: Farm.

THE INTERPRETER: —Farm?

THE WITNESS: Farm.

Q. Farm?

A. Farm.

THE COURT: Farm, f-a-r-m, in English?

MR. ANDERSON: Farm.

MS. GIACCHETTI: Farm.

MR. HALPRIN: Farm.

THE COURT: F-a-r-m?

MR. WOOLEY: F-a-r-m.

THE INTERPRETER: Greenfield Farm.

MR. SCULLY: Farm.

MR. ANDERSON: I'm sorry I brought it up.

And so On, And so On

A. The person who hit the person behind me was the person behind the person behind me. He, having hit the person behind me, the person behind me hit me.

Here We Go Again

Q. Who dropped it?

A. Tony Who.

Q. Which attorney represented you, if you know?

A. Attorney is Who.

Q. Excuse me?

MR. OLIFANT: Counsel, the last name of the attorney who handles the case is Who, much like the routine with which we're so familiar.

Q. Who?

A. Yes.

Q. That was the attorney who represented you?

A. Yes.

Q. Who?

Asked and Answered and Answered

Q. Mr. Smith, I believe your prior testimony before lunch was that you were not arguing with Sam Stevens outside the bar?

A. No.

Q. Is that correct?

A. No, I wasn't.

Q. You were not arguing?

A. No.

Q. Do, you were arguing?

A. No, I wasn't.

Q. You were not arguing?

A. No.

Q. Is it correct that you were not arguing with Mr. Stevens?

A. Yes.

Q. Yes?

Black and White

Q. So there were two supervisors?

A. Yes; White and Black.

THE COURT: Are those the names or ethnic groups?

THE WITNESS: Well, both judge.

Q. OK. So it's Mr. White and Mr. Black and they are black and white?

A. Yeah. One's black and one's white.

THE COURT: Who's Black and who's White?

THE WITNESS: Mr. Black and Mr. White.

THE COURT: No, no. I'm sorry. For example, is Mr. Black black and Mr. White white?

THE WITNESS: Oh, OK. No, Mr. White is black and Mr. Black is white.

THE DEFENDANT: I'm part Apache. Can I get in on this?

Who Do?

Q. Do you know whether or not your daughter has ever been involved in the voodoo or occult?

A. No, I don't know if she practices.

Q. Do you know if she buys any publications on voodoo?

A. We both do.

Q. Voodoo?

A. We do.

Q. You do?

A. Yes, voodoo.

"I firmly believe in the right to a speedy trial."

A Phantom Driver?

Q. As an officer of the Dodge City Police Department, did you stop an automobile bearing Kansas license plates SCR446?

A. Yes, sir.

Q. Was the vehicle occupied at the time you stopped it?

Justifiable Panic

Q. Did the woman driving the car you rear-ended attempt to talk to you?

A. No.

Q. How did you leave the scene of the accident?

A. Scared.

Lost Control of Your Case, Too

Q. Was it a controlled intersection, do you know?

A. I didn't have no control at that intersection; that's why we had the collision.

Almost

Q. Isn't it true that what Mr. Pierce told you is that he almost heard a crunch and then they almost ran over the motor?

Speed Defined

Q. About how long a time was this before the explosion actually occurred?

A. Not too long. Put it like this: By the time I got my feet ready to run, it done gone.

Newton's Law

Q. As you were swooping in on these defendants and you were 45 feet away, how fast were you traveling?

A. I wasn't driving the car. I don't know.

Q. How fast was your partner traveling?

A. I don't know how fast my partner was traveling.

THE COURT: Same speed as you were traveling?

THE WITNESS: Same speed as I was traveling.

How to Eliminate Back Talk
Q. What did you see him do?

A. Saw him having a conversation with a red vehicle. He was on a bicycle.

Did it Hurt?
Q. So your car was injured, for purposes of the record, from the end of the front door back to the bumper?

Logical Question — and Answer
Q. Could you estimate how far that car that swerved in front of the Ford was in front of the Ford before it swerved?

Double Meaning

Q. Did she indicate to you where she was when she witnessed the accident?

A. She was in the southbound lane of the intersection on Karlov, right at the intersection, waiting to cross herself.

Preoccupied

Q. Where was the security officer in relation to you when you were struck by a car?

A. To my left.

Q. How far to your left?

A. I don't really remember. I was getting run over at the time.

Did They Teach That in Driver's Ed?

Q. What did you do to prevent the accident?

A. I just closed my eyes and screamed as loud as I could.

Quite a Feat

A. Well, see, I drive with two feets, right?

Q. OK.

A. So while I was gone down Landis Avenue, I had my feet on the brakes just a little bit, because it was raining. And I had my feet — my other feet, my right feet, on the gas. But as I was coming down and I seen the car coming out of the Jamesway parking lot, I took my feet off the gas, and moved the left feet and put the right feet on the brake.

Personal Observation

THE COURT: Mr. Mulaney, you were supposed to be here on July 7 on this case. And there is nothing much to it, charged with driving with no license validly issued to you — a misdemeanor, but it's not usually a jail case. Your record sucks. How old are you?

THE DEFENDANT: Twenty.

THE COURT: What are you trying to be? A crook?

THE DEFENDANT: No.

THE COURT: Not very good at it either.

Smile

Q. Now, there's a photo on Exhibit 2 you're looking at. Is that how Mr. Thompson appeared on September 28, 1993, with a little bit of a beard like that on his face or—

A. I don't remember him specifically. I remember the driver's license and I remember looking at him and the driver's license because it was one of the most ugliest pictures I'd ever seen on a driver's license.

MR. SMITH: Your Honor, I don't know what to do with that.

MR. JONES: We'll stipulate that was the Department of Motor Vehicle's fault.

Why Bother?

THE COURT: Miss Pitstop, you have got one of the worst driving abstracts I have ever seen, and it is also one of the dumbest driving abstracts I have ever seen because most people lose their driver's license for something more consequential.

Here, you posted your driver's license as bond on a ticket involving disregarding a traffic control device. Then your license was suspended for not showing up in court. There was another suspension for having 10 outstanding parking tickets.

MISS PITSTOP: My car got booted. I never got it back.

THE COURT: Well, that is probably a lucky thing for you. It kept you from getting arrested for a while, but this will be your eighth conviction for driving on a suspended license; and as I said your license was originally suspended just for not showing up in court.

You have some other arrests here for just about everything on the traffic code; following too closely, improper U-turn, violation of seat-belt act, driving without headlights, disregarding traffic control light, disregarding stop sign, driving the wrong way on a one-way street, driving around island, speeding, driving upon sidewalk—

MISS PITSTOP: That's because I can't see without my glasses.

THE COURT: That's comforting.

Blowing the Wrong Horn

Q. Did you blow your horn or anything?

A. After the accident?

Q. Before the accident.

A. Sure, I played for 10 years. I went to school for it and everything.

Under the Influence of a Katzenjammer

Q. You are charged with operating a motor vehicle while under the influence of an alcoholic beverage. Had you been drinking?

A. The night before, uh-huh.

Q. And at the time you were arrested, in your own opinion were you under the influence of an alcoholic beverage?

A. Well, I had a pretty good damn hangover.

Q. Is that the same as being under the influence?

A. Yeah, yeah. It's worse.

All-A Student

Q. And you haven't attended any schools in order to train how to detect nonalcoholic drivers, have you?

Testifying Under the Influence of the Truth

THE COURT: To the charge of driving while intoxicated, how do you plead?

THE DEFENDANT: Drunk.

Has No Problem Drinking

Q. Mr. Meade, do you have a drinking problem?

A. No, I don't.

Q. Have you ever been drunk before?

A. No, I haven't. If I have, I sure don't remember.

Draw Your Own Conclusion

Q. Trooper, was the defendant obviously drunk when you arrested her?

DEFENSE COUNSEL: Objection, your Honor. It calls for a conclusion.

THE COURT: Sustained.

Q. Trooper, when you stopped the defendant were your red and blue lights flashing?

A. Yes, sir.

Q. Did the defendant say anything when she got out of her car?

A. Yes, sir.

Q. What did she say?

A. "What disco am I at."

"Repeat? I Thought You Said Repent!"

Q. How many beers did you drink?
A. One or two.
THE COURT REPORTER: How many?
THE WITNESS: Well, maybe three or four.

Knowing Your Limit

Q. Did they ever serve you more than one drink at a time?
A. No. I can't drink more than one drink at a time.

Witness Says He Doesn't Smell

Q. Do you think if he had a strong odor of alcohol about his breath you would have noticed?
A. No. I can't smell.
Q. Is that for like all the time?
A. Well, it has to be a very, very, very strong odor for me to be able to smell.
Q. I'm sorry to hear that.
A. Working in the jail, sometimes it's an advantage.

Clearly Stated

Q. Where were you?

A. I was in the front right passenger seat.

Q. What state were you in?

A. I was slightly inebriated. I was in good spirits—

Q. Were you in Illinois?

Experience Helps

Q. Officer, you say you are absolutely sure the defendant was intoxicated?

A. Yes, sir.

Q. And how long have you been with the state police?

A. Six months.

Q. And after only six months on the force, you are able to say, to know that the defendant was intoxicated?

A. Well, before I joined the force, I was a bartender for 16 years.

An Ancient Profession

Q. Would you be able to perform any kind of work that you know of right now?

A. Sampling wine.

Alcoholic Confusion

Q. So you could not say one way or the other whether this individual was under the influence of alcohol?

A. No, I can't say that.

Q. Well, it's a double negative. It's true, is it not, that you can't say one way or the other whether this individual was under the influence of alcohol? Do you understand the question?

A. I did the first time. Now I'm confused.

I Beg to Differ

Q. Are you still going to Alcoholics Anonymous?

A. No, sir, that's been about five years ago. I hadn't had no problem with it since. I hadn't drank nothing in two years. I wasn't no alcoholic to start with. Just a plain drunk; everybody has them.

True Eloquence

Q. Now, Officer, besides the flushed face, the weaving motion, the staggering gait and the odor of alcohol emitting from his breath, did you notice anything else unusual about the defendant before you arrested him?

A. Yes. His speech was slick and third — or sick and furled — or, I mean, he was very incoherent.

Q. I understand.

"And you say that all these extra zeros came from your trying to get your ballpoint pen to work?"

Standing Up for Your Beliefs

Q. If after hearing all the evidence in this case there was a reasonable doubt in your mind as to the defendant's guilt, how would you vote?

A. I would vote the way the rest of the jurors did.

Innocence Lost

Q. You didn't tell them that she was a victim of an assault that involved sex and booze?

A. No, I don't believe I did. Possible, yes, possible. No, I can't remember. I know I didn't discuss sex because I didn't know anything about it at that time.

Terminally Tough Neighborhood

Q. And another reason that you didn't want to go out there was because you feared for your life?

A. Yes, I did.

Q. Why?

A. That's a rowdy neighborhood, and there are very, very bad persons that will do bodily harm and seriously kill someone.

Of All Places

Q. Where are your hemorrhoids located?

A. My hemorrhoids? In the posterior.

True Self-Knowledge

Q. Do you believe that you have any expertise at all in the area of construction or design?

That's two separate questions now.

A. Construction, no; design, yes. I may be a very bad designer, but still an expert on bad designing.

Relaxing the Witness

Q. Have you ever had your deposition taken before?

A. No.

Q. Well, it's just like we're sitting in a living room talking, except that you're nervous and I'm not.

Perceptive Juror

Q. What kind of people do you think go free more than others? Do you think people that do drugs and things like that get off, or do you think that people that commit violent crimes like rape and murder, do you think more of those get off, or do you have an opinion?

A. I don't know. I guess probably people with good lawyers get off more than people with bad lawyers.

The Need for Higher Education

A. Even a good thief takes a least 30 or 40 seconds to steal a car, depending on the type of car, without keys.

Q. What does a bad thief take?

A. Could take all day.

Editorializing

Q. I believe that Ms. Dennis, when she was testifying, said something to the effect that she understood there were rumors at some point that she and Mr. Turner were having an affair. Did you hear rumors to that effect?

A. No. Yuck. Excuse me.

I'm Objective — To a Limit

A. I have absolutely, positively no regard for the medical profession, and you may center that, underline it, and dot and dash it. I despise them; I loathe them; I detest them; I find them the scum of the earth. Other than that, I have no problem with them.

The Terminator
Q. Did you ask him to repair the roof?
A. No. At this time he was terminated.
Q. You mean he was dead?
MR. SMITH: We wish.

Ambitious Hobbyist
Q. What are your hobbies?
A. Drinking coffee and watching girls.

Definition of Stingy
Q. Do you know if he paid the person who came in and poured the concrete?
A. I've never seen John Knight spend a dime. He holds a nickel so tight the Indian is riding on the buffalo's back.

"I Am Not a Crook"

Q. You were out there on a weekend. You were doing target shooting?

A. Yes.

Q. What were you shooting at?

A. A newspaper with a picture of President Nixon on it.

Q. At least you knew what to shoot at.

Definition of Nonfight

A. Well, see, what happened is I couldn't do my job, and this guy I was working with felt he was pulling the load, and it just kind of got out of hand. But as far as the physical fight went, it wasn't a fight. Do you know what I mean?

Q. No physical contact between the two of you then?

A. Well, it was physical contact, but I guess he must have gotten the physical part of it, you know, because he never touched me.

Q. You hit him but he didn't hit you?

A. Right. He swung and missed; I didn't.

Descriptive Witness

A. My impression of one of the meanings of a vulture fund is a fund that is established for the purpose of acquiring assets that are severely depressed, much the same as a vulture might pick the bones of a carcass that has ripened well.

Q. What a lovely analogy.

Boorish Behavior

PROSECUTOR: Your Honor, it seems the defendant got into a fight with her husband, who is the plaintiff's brother. All the plaintiff wants is an apology; she just wants the defendant to admit she was wrong to break the window.

THE DEFENDANT: I'm sorry I broke the window.

THE COURT: Do you two think you can still be friends now?

THE DEFENDANT: Yes.

THE PLAINTIFF: Yes, your Honor.

THE COURT: Because, you know, I can tell you two care about each other. You were very good friends; and then some man comes along and messes it all up. Now, don't you always be siding with your brother, because you know he's a lout.

Straightforward Judge

THE COURT: This is what I'm going to do, Mr. Kosteleski. I'm going to give you a continuance to November 16. When you come back on that date, if you haven't taken care of everything on this case, you should say a little prayer before you come in the room. That prayer should be: "Oh, please God, make it not be the same judge who's on the bench." Because frankly, my friend, if this was still my regular court, you would go to jail today.

THE DEFENDANT: Exactly, the 16th.

What About Off the Record?

Q. There was some discussion about Mickey's bed-wetting activities before the wreck. Has he improved at all?

A. As he gets older, yeah, it's improved.

Q. I'm no expert, but I assume most kids grow out of that.

MR. OLIVER: You did, right?

MR. GREGORY: On the record, I will say that I did.

THE WITNESS: We got that, right?

(Reporter nodded head.)

Attitude

Q. Can you characterize the meeting for me in terms of was it cordial, was it an interrogation, was it forceful? Tell me about it.

A. Well, the first meeting was loose or friendly in the beginning. Then it started to become somewhat of an interrogation. Then they started throwing questions at me from both angles and it was not cordial at all.

Q. Not cordial? Did you feel intimidated?

A. Well, they tried to, but I'm a New Yorker and we don't get intimidated.

Just the Facts, Please

Q. Right; just so I understand, it doesn't hurt when you have sex?

A. No, it doesn't hurt.

Q. OK.

A. Feels good sometimes.

Failing in School

A. His attempt to make a friendship with teachers in order to have the academic load lessened suggests that his social behavior is pretty inappropriate.

Q. So anybody that tries to brownnose a teacher has got a problem?

A. You betcha, if it doesn't work.

All in a Day's Work

A. I worked in cemeteries.

Q. What did you do there?

A. Redecorate the cemetery. Like dig up bodies when they were through. When your lot ran out, I dig up bodies and put the bones in something, and they take them and store them. I don't know what they do with them. Pick the gold out of them and get rid of them. I don't know.

Q. Moving right along—

An Honest Criminal

THE COURT: What is your occupation?

THE DEFENDANT: I'm a thief.

THE COURT: Thief. I see. How's business?

THE DEFENDANT: It's a little slow right now.

THE COURT: And how do you get along when you are not working at your usual occupation?

THE DEFENDANT: I'm usually in prison.

THE COURT: I see.

True Honesty

Q. What can you tell us about the truthfulness and veracity of this defendant?

A. Oh, she will tell the truth. She said she'd kill the son of a bitch — and she did it.

An Honest Response

Q. Good afternoon. Mr. Clark, how many times have you been convicted of a felony or crime involving dishonesty or false statement?

A. Never.

Q. Pardon?

A. False statement?

Q. How many times have you been convicted of a felony or a crime involving false statement or dishonesty?

A. You make more than one question.

Q. Yes. How many times, explain it if you want.

A. OK, let me explain that. I have been convicted for three felony, three felony. I never have been convicted of any crime of dishonesty, never have lied, never have been charged with any, committing any perjury in my life.

Slight Resemblance

Q. And what did you see when [the accused] pulled down his pants?

A. It looked like a penis, only smaller.

A Good Answer

Q. When was the first time you dropped out of class because of fatigue or memory problems?

A. I don't recall. I can't remember.

Going Solo

Q. Was anyone in the restroom at the time of your accident?

A. No, sir. Again, I have to tell you, I don't take anybody in the restroom when I go.

MURPHY'S LAWYER

And See What the Bulls in the Back Room Will Have

Q. Just by its very nature, weren't they purchasing older cattle, cattle that were inebriated and had other different problems with them?

A. No.

Q. Were the older cattle that were being bought for cow kills more susceptible to disease, more inebriated than the cows you could find in a fat cow kill?

A. No.

THE COURT: Is that the word: "inebriated"?

MR. SMITH: That's true.

MR. JONES: Emaciated.

MR. SMITH: Emaciated.

MR. DOE: Inebriated? Judge, I think he confused attorneys with cows there when he was talking about inebriated.

Why We Hire Lawyers

Q. Did you tell your son that you were going to cut Carolyn's liver out?

A. No. I told him I was going to let my attorney take care of that.

Reuben to Go

Q. How did you choose Mr. Reuben as your attorney? Did you know his name? Or did you get it out of the phone book?

MR. REUBEN: That is totally irrelevant. You may go ahead and answer, but it's totally irrelevant. If you know the answer, go ahead and answer it.

A. I had a list of Indianapolis attorneys and — don't laugh when I tell you this — but I like reuben sandwiches.

Sure You Want a Jury Trial?

MR. MARTIN: This may sound like a preemptive strike. I know I am boring, Judge, but I already have one fast asleep. She is still sleeping, if you look over there now, one of the jurors.

THE COURT: Is there a rule that jurors have to stay awake?

MR. MARTIN: I think there is something about I am entitled to 12 reasonably competent jurors. I didn't want to go over there and yell in her ear or anything, but she is out like a light.

THE COURT: What do you suggest that I do?

MR. MARTIN: Maybe another brief recess or something.

THE COURT: We just got back from a recess.

MR. MARTIN: I don't know. This lady must be very tired.

MR. ROTHMAN: How about nap time or something?

MR. MARTIN: Milk and cookies?

MR. BRANDT: I had a juror sleep through a trial last year, and it was a murder trial.

THE COURT: Has she changed any at all?

MR. MARTIN: She turned her head and is sleeping on the other side so as not to get a crick in her neck.

MS. CONNORS: Why don't you ask the jury to stand up?

MR. MARTIN: I am entitled to 12 alive jurors. This woman may be dead for all I know.

MS. CONNORS: For purposes of the record, she has been moving from side to side.

MR. MARTIN: Judge, take a look.

MS. CONNORS: She just moved.

THE COURT: Let's get going.

Non Sequitur of the Week

Q. What doctors have you spoken to about your tinnitus?

A. Hey, it's snowing out there.

Prudent Driver

Q. Are you a believer in seat belts?

A. Yeah.

Q. To what extent? Do you recommend seat belts to your family and friends and everyone to whom you speak?

A. Oh, I recommend — every lawyer that sits in my car should have a seat belt on.

Punny Lawyer

Q. When you don't have a heavy activity day, do your shoulders and neck bother you?

A. Depends on really what type of errands I'm doing. I generally take care of all the business, and if I sit there on a straight chair and figure out all the bills and stuff like that for a length of time, that always bothers my shoulders.

Q. Bills are a pain in the neck to everyone.

Can I Get a Rimshot, Please?

Q. That's 4-G.

A. However, in the picture you can barely make out here—

MR. BAILEY: For the record, 4-I.

MR. HENSLEY: Just because I wear glasses, don't insult me.

MR. BAILEY: It took me a minute.

A Good One to Forget

Q. Have you ever been convicted of a felony?

A. Yes.

Q. What felony?

A. I shot a guy. You was my lawyer. Have you forgot.

I Changed Majors

Q. I take it at some point you concluded that you would attend law school instead of medical school?

A. I thought I'd try to make a living with my mouth instead of my brain.

Priorities

Q. What happened next?

A. He stated that they were both bare-skinned from the waist up, and she proceeded to give him a back massage from the top on down to the tailbone and at some point had rubbed across his crotch area and aroused him. And then he asked for an attorney.

Two Courses of Action

MS. ALBERTS: As the judge indicated, my name is Laura Alberts and I'm representing Mr. and Mrs. Tenely along with Victor Henry.

This is called voir dire, and this is my opportunity to speak with you as jurors. After this point in the trial, I won't have any opportunity to ask you any questions or to have any intercourse with you.

Discourse.

I didn't mean that.

THE COURT: And we send them to law school to learn all these words.

MS. ALBERTS: I apologize for that.

THE COURT: Wait just a minute.

Terry, I'd like to have a transcript of that please.

Doctor, Diagnose Thyself

Q. Doctor, could stress lead to further symptoms?

A. Stress is a definitive mechanism of chest pain, yes, sir. For me, the greatest cause of chest pain is lawyers.

That Was No Gentleman; That Was My Lawyer

A. And the person in the picture that the gentleman showed you — that the lawyer showed you — was the same person who was injured.

Painful Question

Q. Other than that, the swelling has gone down, and the only residual is the headaches you have given me?

Setting Priorities

Q. You said he threatened to kill you?

A. Yes. And he threatened to sue me.

Q. Oh, worse yet.

Well, You Asked

Q. Earlier in the deposition you said you lost the tip of a finger in a blender accident; is that correct?

A. Uh-huh, yes.

Q. May I ask which finger.

A. (Indicating)

Q. You thoroughly enjoyed that, didn't you, ma'am?

Body Language

Q. With regard to your philosophy or perception of life or existence, are you familiar with the term "eternal verities"?

A. "Eternal verities"? Isn't that more of a legal term?

Q. Not from the expression on your attorney's face.

A Fool for an Attorney?

A. It would be very foolhardy for an attorney to involve his client in an affair such as that without getting collateral to secure the payment.

Q. And without being facetious, but you are not a foolhardy attorney, right?

MR. HOWELL: Objection, your Honor.

THE COURT: We'll take judicial note of that.

MR. HOWELL: And we have so stipulated.

THE WITNESS: Has it been stipulated that I am or am not a foolhardy attorney?

THE COURT: I'm not sure. We'll see.

THE WITNESS: My presence here today leads me to wonder.

Even More Insulting

Q. How did you get the impression that he was mad? You said he insulted you for a while, by that he called you a lawyer, I mean a liar?

MR. MILLER: I will object to that, your Honor.

Q. OK. He called you a liar, and he said that you were no good. How else did he insult you?

A. Well, that's enough for me.

Q. That's enough for you?

A. Yeah.

Q. It's a good thing he didn't call you a lawyer.

Off to a Bad Start

Q. Ma'am, the reason we're here today—

A. Yes, I know why we're here, but make yourself a little bit more understandable, so I can understand you. I have a very hard time understanding sometimes, so make it a little bit more understandable for me since you're the lawyer in this case.

Q. Do you want me to act like a lawyer?

A. No, sir. I want you to act like a human being.

New Parenthetical Needed

MR. SMITH: The record should reflect heavy eye contact between the client and counsel.

Time Takes its Toll

Q. We've been at this too long. It's time for a break.

A. You're telling me.

Q. Hey, I've been at this for 19 years.

A. This case has been going on for 19 years?

MR. JONES: Feels like it.

MR. SMITH: No. I've been practicing law for 19 years.

THE WITNESS: You call this practicing law?

A Lawyer With a Sense of Humor

MR. THOMAS: Could we have a spelling of the street, please?

MR. JOHNSON: W-o-o-d-b-i-n-e.

MR. THOMAS: Does your lawyer know how to spell?

THE WITNESS: I believe so.

MR. JOHNSON: Just up to the w's.

Mixing Adjectives

DEFENSE ATTORNEY: Did he tell you he had the ability to see the man's face?

POLICE DETECTIVE: He said that when the defendant was in the store he had a scarf over his mouth. When he started chasing him and the defendant got nervous, the scarf fell down. Resolutely he saw the defendant's face.

DEFENSE ATTORNEY: What do you mean, "Resolutely he saw the defendant's face"?

POLICE DETECTIVE: Don't worry about adverbs. It's just "resolutely." It's, in other words, as a result. I'll keep it simple. I'm sorry.

DEFENSE ATTORNEY: Thank you.

Memorable Quip

Q. What problems were you having with your memory? You hadn't mentioned that earlier.

A. I believe I did. I'm sorry. If I didn't, I thought I had.

Q. Must have forgot.

Maybe He Stubbed His Coma Toes

Q. Was he unconscious before or after he said he was hurt?

A. He was unconscious after he said he was hurt.

MR. DANIELS: Either that or he had more capability unconscious than you or I do.

Out of Reach

Q. Do you maintain employment records on your employees, and would you have a last known address on Nishon?

A. He's either in heaven or hell. He's deceased.

Q. That narrows things down. Thank you.

MR. ALLEN: He's beyond subpoena power.

The Frito Defense

Q. You assumed narcotics in reaching your opinions.

A. Yes.

Q. You didn't assume a Frito or a Chee-to or a banana. You assumed narcotics.

A. It was a narcotics raid. It wasn't a Frito raid, counselor.

Defensive Witness

MR. SMITH: It may very well have affected or conceivably affected his emotional and mental state.

THE WITNESS: I've heard everything now. Are you saying I'm mental? I want an apology from you.

MS. HAYES: That is not what Mr. Smith is saying.

THE WITNESS: Where did the mental come from? Tell him to rephrase it right. After all, he's a lawyer.

Reporting at the Zoo

Q. Mrs. Bryant, my name is Richard Jones, and I represent Mr. Smith in this matter.

A. OK.

Q. Did I read in these reports that you had trouble hearing?

A. A little bit sometimes.

Q. Am I talking loud enough now?

A. It's the pitch of your voice that bothers me. If you sound like a bird or a frog, I can't hear you.

Q. Do I sound like either?

A. I would say you're coming across like a panda.

Q. Well, OK. I'm going to ask you some questions today and if you don't hear me or if my voice turns into that of a bird vs. a panda, let me know and I'll try to change that.

MR. DOE: As best you can, tweet, tweet.

MR. JONES: Yes, as best I can.

Motion of the Foot Granted

THE COURT: What's the problem?

THE BAILIFF: Oh, a cockroach was on the exhibit table, your Honor.

PLAINTIFF'S COUNSEL: Motion to quash.

THE COURT: Granted.

Secret Testimony

Q. You're the Ross of Ross & Cohen?

A. Yes.

Q. Would that mean you're the senior partner of the firm?

A. I'm one of them.

THE COURT: You're what?

THE WITNESS: I'm one of them. Mr. Cohen wouldn't want to hear I'm the only one.

THE COURT: We won't tell him.

Witness Encouraged to Edit

(After the witness gave a long, rambling answer:)

MR. PIRO: Do you see how easy it would have been if you just said "stock."

THE WITNESS: Bob, I have to process these things through my mind.

MR. PIRO: But the processing doesn't have to be coming out of your mouth.

Yoo Hoo, Yahoo

MR. JACOBS: Don't wave at me, or I will wave at you.

MR. NORTH: You did wave.

MR. JACOBS: You can wave and I'll wave. Why don't we take five minutes to wave at each other.

MR. BLACK: Why don't we stipulate that all waves will be waived.

Play Ball!

Q. Having reviewed the charge and being able — strike that.

At the time — strike that. I'm getting tired.

MR. SMITH: One more strike and you're out.

Solitary Confinement

Q. Whether you wish to plead guilty or not is up to you.

A. Going by the advice of counsel, I will plead guilty.

Q. Do you understand your counsel is not going to spend any time in jail?

A. I know that. It would be nice to have the company.

Outside the Court's Jurisdiction

Q. And is there anyone who can corroborate what was said in that meeting, to your knowledge, other than you, your lawyer and Mr. Smith here?

A. Outside of God, I can't think of anybody else.

Q. Well, I don't think I have the ability to produce him as a witness.

A. I don't either.

An English Lesson

Q. Where did you talk to him?

A. On the phone.

Q. Did he call you or did you call him?

A. I called him.

Q. What number did you call him?

A. I called him "David." I don't call him a number.

Q. What number did you call him?

MR. NORTH: At.

THE WITNESS: Never end a sentence in a preposition.

Courtroom Clowning

MR. LEVINE: That's a yes-or-no question. It's really not that difficult.

MR. ELLIOT: Well, that's a bozo question.

MR. LEVINE: No it's not.

MR. ELLIOT: It's a total bozo question.

MR. LEVINE: Do you want to discuss it outside?

MR. ELLIOT: No. It's a bozo question. If you want to answer it, go ahead.

MR. LEVINE: I assume you are calling me a bozo.

MR. ELLIOT: I'm saying the question is bozotic.

THE WITNESS: Say it again, please.

MR. LEVINE: Can she read back the question before the references to bozos.

Press and Twist, If You Can

MR. SMITH: I don't know whether I'm smart enough to open this or not.

MR. JONES: Probably not. It's childproof.

MR. SMITH: Aren't you funny.

116

Early Legal Training

Q. I can't throw away this beautiful exhibit that I worked on so diligently this afternoon, finally getting to utilize skills that I picked up in the third and fourth grades.

I Don't Want to Be Here When ...

A. Service meaning that you know what — you have to know what you're doing. You're dealing with expensive equipment. If I go in there and I don't know what the heck I'm doing, I'm going to be in deep trouble.

MR. THOMAS: That's a legal phrase, too.

MR. GREEN: Deep trouble?

MR. THOMAS: Yes.

MR. GREEN: It's related to a more significant legal phrase that involves certain materials hitting the fan.

"No, you can't break a deadlock by doing 'rock, paper and scissors.'"

One Track Mind
Q. Now, when did you move into 603 Apple Street?
A. March of '84.
Q. Had you ever lived anywhere else before?

Let Me Start Again
MR. GRIFFIN: What was the question?
Q. Sir, the question is, it says here — could you tell me, then, first of all, I guess the question is, was that an accurate statement?
A. Repeat the question. I lost you.

Punny Question

Q. Can yeast infections give rise to anything else that you are aware of?

There's a Sensitive Soul Under That Hard-Boiled Exterior

Q. I'm really trying to determine whether it is your claim that any of the things set forth in your petition, and in particular the claims set forth in Mr. Jones' letter of February 15, 1984, are things that you could not have discovered during the period from October 13, 1982, to March 11, 1983, that you could not have discovered—

Now I got myself ass backwards. I couldn't answer that myself. All right.

MR. JONES: Are you going to have him read it back?

MR. SMITH: No, hell, no. Let's start over again. I would hate to listen to it again.

Brown Eyes

Q. Can you look through these pictures and tell me how many brown eyes are in there?

A. Three.

Q. Of those people with the three brown eyes, how many people have a distinctive mustache?

A. (No reply)

Q. Of the three people with the three brown eyes—

A. Of the people with the three brown eyes?

Q. Please.

Somebody Get a Camera!

Q. In addition to that, it's my understanding from talking to you that you had problems dressing. For example, if you are going out, to pull your pantyhose on your husband would — you had to lay down and he would wiggle you into them?

Then Stop Complaining

Q. So your only complaint about being given that sales territory was that you were beaten and robbed?

A. No, not beaten. I was just robbed.

Focusing on the Issue

Q. Were you using any means to enhance your ability to observe what was transpiring?

A. Huh?

THE COURT: Were you using binoculars?

To Ask or Not to Ask

Q. When did you start to next intend to look — let me strike that. It seems so bad that it was almost Shakespeare.

"Say What?" Dept.

Q. Of the types of things you said that you were looking for, what types of things do those things that you were looking for relate to insofar as things go?

What Was the Question?

Q. These are two different reports for the two different quarters?

A. Correct.

Q. I apologize and withdraw the question that I didn't ask to avoid confusion that didn't occur.

MR. JONES: I'm not so sure it didn't occur.

THE WITNESS: Now I'm confused.

A Revealing Question

Q. What type of clothing is indigenous to Wal-Mart? What do sales clerks wear, if anything?

Shooting for the Bull's-Eye

PROSECUTING ATTORNEY: Is there anyone not here who could just not convict the defendant because you just don't want to convict anyone?

Let Me Rephrase

Q. Have you ever talked with a gentleman named Malcolm Miller?

A. No.

Q. Ever talked with a person named Malcolm Miller who was not a gentleman?

Violence in the Courtroom

MR. SMITH: That's vague, overbroad, burdensome and the question ought to be taken out and shot.

MR. BROWN: As long as we don't shoot the questioner.

Huh?

Q. It is possible that you could have spoken with Cathy LaSota prior to July 12 of 1989 regarding her conversation with Kevin Mulqueen and do not recall it presently?

MS. COHEN: Don't answer, Loretta. That can't be answered. That's nonsense.

MR. ARAPS: That is a perfectly legitimate question.

MS. COHEN: You're questioning her as to whether or not she can recall that what she doesn't recollect now, she may have had a conversation for which she has no recollection, but she may have it anyway in spite of her recollection that she has no recollection.

MR. ARAPS: You understand very well.

Do You Know?

Q. Do you know if you ever did know—

MR. SMITH: That's a good question.

Q. —even though you don't recall now what it was?

MR. SMITH: He's just asking you if you know if you ever did know.

Yum Yum

Q. We're just talking regular lettuce as opposed to ptomaine?

MS. WARDELL: Not ptomaine, romaine.

You Lost Him

Q. Now, sir, did you or did you not on the date in question, or at any other time previously or subsequently, say, or even intimate, to the defendant or anyone else, alone or with anyone, whether friend or mere acquaintance, or, in fact, a stranger, that the statement imputed to you, whether just or unjust, and denied by the plaintiff, was a matter of no importance, or otherwise? Answer yes or no.

A. Yes or no what?

No Room for Logic

Q. As far as you know today, there is nothing about that statement that is untrue?

A. For those other people, it is not. If we're going to use logic on this, then I would have to start doubting. Because, if it doesn't work for us, if it didn't work for my brother, and he says it works for everyone, then that raises the question: Did it work for everybody that he said it worked for?

Q. Well, to the extent we can, let's resist the temptation of being logical and just answer questions.

Excuse Me?

Q. So that isn't correct; is that correct?

Twosome

Q. When one of you rides with the other, I suppose you are in the same vehicle at the same time?

A. Yes.

Sorry, I Must've Dozed Off

Q. The question is simply designed to have you reflect for a moment and think if there is anything that stands out in your mind that in any way leads you to believe that you are not required to give an answer in whole to or in part to the pending question and all you are required to do is give me your firsthand impression of your firm belief right now as to whether any such fact or belief occurs to you as you sit here and think about it, as I am sure that you understand the question, but if you are in the least bit confused, or if there is some word that there is some doubt about, I will have the reporter read the question and you can ask for clarification. OK?

Clarifying Matters

MR. JONES: May I ask for a clarification? You're not asking whether or not he believes today that his then understanding was correct but simply whether at the time when he looked at it and thought he didn't understand it as opposed to thinking he understood it but understood it incorrectly?

Precision
Q. 2:30 a.m., that's in the morning?
A. Yes.

It Usually Helps
Q. Were you present when specimens were taken from you in the conduct of this examination?
A. Yes.

It Figures
Q. How old are her children?
A. Eight and seven.
Q. Which one is the older?
A. Eight.
Q. I can follow that.

Pay Attention, Counsel

Q. And the youngest son, the 20-year-old, how old is he?
A. He is 20 years old.

It Goes Without Saying

Q. So you were gone until you returned?

Ask a Stupid Question ...

Q. Do you remember when Sunday was that week?
A. Well, yes, I assume it followed Saturday.

What Else Is There?

Q. I notice you're wearing glasses. Are you nearsighted, shortsighted or do you just wear those for reading?

Witness Simplifies Question

Q. And what is the name of your employment there as far as hourly rate and financial reimbursement?

A. You mean how much do I make an hour?

Q. Yes.

What Do You Think

Q. When an officer went over to where this fight was taking place at the corner of the house, what were those people fighting doing?

A. Fighting.

I Hope So

Q. Now, did you have any children with Richard?

A. Yes, three boys.

Q. Do you remember their names?

Digging for Facts
Q. And all the items included in that photograph — were they present at the time that photograph was taken?
A. Yes, sir.

Attendance Required
Q. Were you conceived prior to your father leaving, or were you conceived after your father left?
MR. HARTER: I don't know if that works.

The Case of the Wandering Mind
Q. Can you describe that individual?
A. He was about medium height and had a beard.
Q. Was this a male or female?

Clarification
Q. I understand you recently gave birth to twins?
A. Yes, ma'am.
Q. That's two babies?
A. Yes, twins.

Getting a Good Look
Q. How were you making the distinction?
A. Objective process.
Q. Which is what kind of process?
A. Examination, optical examination.
Q. Does that mean you looked at it?
A. Yes.

You Asked for It
Q. Mr. Johnson, you're looking at the document. Can you tell me what you're looking at?
A. The document.

Asking the Obvious
Q. For what reason do you wear eyeglasses?
A. Can't see very well.

What Do You Think?
Q. Have you ever tried to commit suicide?
A. Yes, sir.
Q. Were you ever successful?
A. No, sir.

Some Might Call it Rude
Q. All right. OK. In the hypothetical you recall we were talking about Mr. Lewis' reaction to the situation. Was it your opinion he had an appropriate reaction to hit somebody in the teeth with a baseball bat?

Do They Think Before They Talk?

Q. What happened then?

A. He told me, he says, "I have to kill you because you can identify me."

Q. Did he kill you?

A. No.

Duh

Q. Are you married, sir?

A. Yes.

Q. And to whom are you married?

A. My wife.

Gee, Let Me Think

Q. Did he ever kill you before?

A. Pardon me?

Timely Response
Q. How recently had you seen Dr. Mostellos?
A. Prior to his death?
Q. Well, yes.

Good Guess
Q. OK. I presume nobody who dies ever contested this?
A. Right.

Talk About Obvious
Q. Were you hurt in that?
A. Ninety-two stitches, 93, whatever.
Q. Where did you go — Did you have to go to an emergency room? I guess you did.
A. Yes.

Our Innocent Lawyers

Q. Do you know how far pregnant you are right now?

A. I will be three months November 8.

Q. Apparently, then, the date of conception was August 8?

A. Yes.

Q. What were you and your husband doing at that time?

Consistent

Q. Doctor, how many autopsies have you performed on dead people?

A. All my autopsies have been on dead people.

Persistence

Q. You don't know what it was, and you don't know what it looked like, but can you describe it?

A. No.

Whodunit Dept.

Q. Did you know he did it when he did it?

A. I don't remember.

Q. Did you know he was going to do it before he did it?

A. I don't remember that either.

Q. Did you learn he had done it after he did it?

A. I don't feel I can accurately answer this.

Enough Said

Q. Anything else?

A. I forget things a lot.

Q. Anything else?

A. I don't remember.

Forgetful

Q. This myasthenia gravis, does it affect your memory at all?

A. Yes.

Q. And in what ways does it affect your memory?

A. I forget.

Q. You forget. Can you give us an example of something that you've forgotten that you can pinpoint that's been caused by this disease?

A. That I forgot?

Q. Yes.

A. I couldn't tell you. I can't remember what I've forgot.

Just a Little Taste, Please?

Q. Did he share meals with you?

A. Did he share meals with me?

Q. On that trip.

A. What do you mean; buy me a meal?

Q. Share meals with you, have meals with you.

A. Like eat off my plate of something?

In Spirit Only

Q. It is your understanding that on your mother's death the land goes to you. You mean she does not have a right to live there anymore, right?

A. Yes.

Dumb Questions Dept.

Q. Do you recall approximately when Grandma told you that?

A. No.

Q. It would have been before Grandma died?

We'll Stipulate to That

Q. And there you're saying because she's dead she's no longer alive; is that what you're saying?

MR. MATTHEWS: Is there a dispute there?

Wondering or Wandering?

Q. Where does John live?

A. He lives in Queens, New York.

Q. He's your twin brother?

A. Yes.

Q. Is he still alive?

A. Yes.

"Judge Brickell discourages long-winded arguments."

The Long Way Around

Q. What time of the day or evening did the accident happen?

A. (From a witness who had earlier loudly declared that he hoped the deposition wouldn't take too long, as he was a very busy man.) Well, it was between 6 and 7, I'd say.

I'm always up around 5 in the morning, shower, shave, have a cup of coffee, sometimes I eat a bowl of cereal, kiss my wife good-bye, gather up my briefcase and paperwork, which I take home every night, load it in the car, back out of the driveway, go north on Rimpau half a block to Eighth, go to the first block, which I guess is Muirfield — I'm sorry, North. It's the east boundary of the big state farm building there, which takes up the whole block. Anyway, it's that east street there. It's in the deposition I previously gave you, or made up.

And I make from there — that dead-ends into Wilshire — I make there a right turn onto Wilshire. I then change lanes, go into the center lane, because Muirfield dead-ends into Wilshire on the north side of Wilshire, and there is a left-turn lane there, which I veer into from the center lane.

And I then make a left turn going north onto Muirfield, which has a stop sign on Muirfield for traffic to stop as they come to turn onto Wilshire for either direction.

Q. You certainly saved a lot of questions.

Throw Him a Life Preserver

Q. Let me ask this question and this is the question so when we come down to the time we have to read this part of the deposition, the question will start here, OK. And the question — hell, what was I thinking about?

Stand While You Sit

A. I felt that's what I was including in my 1988 figures and, as I sit here today, I still stand by that.

Let Me Make This Perfectly Clear

MR. CONNELL: I'm asking a question. It's rather long. But since I was confused before, I want to make sure that my confusion is clear.

Follow These Directions

A. I think "authorized by me" means that he authorized me to do something. And if he directed an investment manager authorized by him to do something, then that investment manager is authorized under his direction to do that. And if you insert me as the investment manager and he directed me, the investment manager, to do something, his direction authorizes me, the investment manager, to do something; then I, the investment manager, am then authorized to do it because he directed me to do it. And at that same time, because I am following his directions to follow my direction, then I can do it.

Small Wonder

A. I'm really not clear on your question, sir.

Q. Well, let me try again. If this letter of intent merely reiterates your earlier agreement, your oral agreement that you refer to, and if the letter of intent and your earlier oral agreement, both, presumably, say we will not be, but this letter does, the agreement does not create any legal obligations, and any legal obligations will be set forth in definitive agree-

ments to be executed, and so no such agreements were executed, then how can Mr. Jackson or you be held responsible because there was no closing? That was part of your oral agreement. You had to have it in writing. And it wasn't in writing. Did you understand that?

A. I'm sorry, sir. I don't understand the question. No, sir.

Q. Well, I'll go ahead. I can't explain it any better than that.

Too Specific

Q. And you said it was very tender?

A. Yes.

Q. Was it actually tender?

A. Yes.

Q. What does that mean?

A. Well, it was very tender.

Brevity and Coherence

Q. If I could draw your attention to this advertisement, it would seem to me as if in your advertisement on the exhibit — we're still referring to the exhibit attached to the complaint — that you have a — I would say quite a bit of the advertisement describes the activities of the club. In fact, there's — you spend quite a few lines. In fact, I'll count them — 11 lines where you describe giveaways for — actually more lines — where you get into the giveaways for the Pocono weekend, this hot holiday bash, descriptive materials of which may be of the nature that you described the differences you have with your wife in terms of formatting these advertisements, the artistic tension, the tension between artistic design and information?

A. I'm not too sure what you're asking.

Continuance, Please

MR. SIMPSON: Your Honor, may it please the Court, this originally was assigned to Mr. Anderson, which is neither here nor there. I took the case over last week.

THE COURT: Mr. Anderson is neither here nor there? If he's not here, he's got to be there.

MR. SIMPSON: You would think, although of late I wonder.

THE COURT: OK. Well, I didn't mean to interrupt you.

MR. SIMPSON: Be that as it may, I am here. However, our witness, Agent Baker, is there. And that is our problem.

Growing Impatient

A. I think maybe at some point in the future I'll be able to say.

Q. Would you be willing to fill in a blank in your deposition that we left and you fill it in 10 years from now?

A. I believe this deposition will still be going on 10 years from now.

MR. FIELD: Not on my dime.

Would You Mind Repeating That?

Q. And then Tracy owed Brown money, correct?

A. Tracy owed Brown money because Tracy had sold the Reppel Steel business to some people who were introduced to Tracy as a result of some other people that Brown had introduced to Tracy when he was trying to sell the land to them.

Q. OK. So at the time your house was busted you really didn't know him that well?

A. I would not say that.

Q. You wouldn't say that?

A. No, sir. I would say that right now I know him as well as I have ever known him, and that is a lot better than I knew him then, but I did know him.

Making it Perfectly Clear

Q. Are you able to answer the question as I have put it?

A. Yes.

MS. BRADY: Well, it's been—

MR. ALLEN: I will ask you to read the question—

THE WITNESS: Could you hold it a second? I am not trying to be evasive.

Q. You may not be understanding—

THE WITNESS: Do you keep writing this down?

THE REPORTER: Until someone says off the record.

MR. ALLEN: We can go off the record.

MS. BRADY: No, let's not go off the record. It might help clarify things.

Looks Like

Q. If at any time you'd like to look at this — in fact, I'd like you to look at this — will you just look at this — well, you can look at this, if you like.

A. Look at this or that?

A Verbal Habit You Know

A. He said he liked East Texas and he — you know, he was reading my application, and he asked me was I interested in, you know, in working that type of work. You know, he would, you know, asked me did I think I could, you know, do the — you know, know how to, you know, work there and do the job, you know, do I think I could, you know, work.

Makes Sense to You, Maybe

A. The process is to convert, utilizing, again, Newton, gravity and converting through the mass times the acceleration rate to equal the energy dissipated to convert from feet per second to miles per hour so that we can end up with an equation that makes sense to us.

A Sharp Mind

(The court had just admonished counsel to hurry things along.)

Q. Without belaboring the point, please state your name.

Biblical Citation

MR. HUNTER: Isn't the saying "Blessed are the peacemakers: for they are the children of God," and "Blessed are the meek: for they—" Do they inherit the earth?

THE COURT: I'm not sure.

MR. HUNTER: I believe they do.

THE COURT: There is a bible in chambers. What's the citation?

That's What She Said, Isn't It?

Q. How far away is your apartment from your husband's?

A. Just a hop, skip and a jump.

Q. Since this is a court of law, we have to be a little more specific because we all jump different distances.

A. Maybe 30 feet.

Q. Using anything in this courtroom, how far would it be if it falls into that category?

A. About from here to the wall, I would say.

THE COURT: That's about a hop, skip and a jump.

Three on a Bed

Q. When the three of you have put your heads together, and you've listened to what they've had to say, and they've listened to what you've had to say, have you come to the opinion in listening to what they've had to say that none of the three of you know what caused the accident to happen; that is, none of the three of you are able to figure out why it was that the bed fell?

Talk, Talk, Talk

Q. Now, you've previously indicated that you could not have done this, you could not have done that because she was not talking to you and could not talk to you, but, in fact, she was talking to you when she told you she could not talk to you, was she not?

A. Well, she was talking to me, telling me she couldn't talk to me. She would have to talk to me to tell me that she couldn't talk to me. After she told me that she couldn't talk to me—

Q. Well, that's again, your assumption. She could have written to you and said she could not talk to you, could she not?

A. Mr. Elkins, there's a point of ridiculousness.

Q. What I'm asking you is, isn't it true that she was talking to you at the time she told you that she couldn't talk to you?

A. No. That is not true. It was a guttural utterance that barely qualified according to the syntax of proper language.

The Price Is Right

THE COURT: The question is: Do you remember? If you don't remember, it's not a problem.

THE WITNESS: I don't remember exactly, no.

Q. Do you know whether it was more than $400?

A. Yes, it was more than $400.

Q. Do you know whether it was more than a thousand dollars?

A. Yes, it was more than a thousand dollars.

Q. Do you know whether it was more than $2,000?

A. Yes, it was.

Q. Was it more than $2,500?

A. Yes.

THE COURT: What is this, "The Price is Right"?

"No" What I Mean?

Q. Have you ever been arrested?

A. No.

Q. The answer is "no."

A. "No."

What's in a Name?

THE COURT: This case is titled *State vs. Johnny Dwight Jenkins.* Is that you correct name?

THE DEFENDANT: No, sir. It is Johnny Duane Jenkins.

THE COURT: How do you spell it?

THE DEFENDANT: I am not for sure, sir.

THE PUBLIC DEFENDER: He is not sure.

THE DEFENDANT: I don't never use my middle name anyway.

THE COURT: You don't know how to spell your middle name?

THE DEFENDANT: No, sir, I don't.

THE COURT: Well, we will just correct it to read a middle initial D.

THE DEFENDANT: Yes, sir.

Layman's Language

Q. How is that calculation performed, if you can explain it so the jury can understand it. I know it's difficult.

A. It's not that difficult. There is an equation called the perfect-gas law, which says pressure times the volume is equal to a constant times the mass times the temperature of a gas.

Using the perfect-gas law, if you know the volume of the containment, you know the free volume built in, so you measure the pressure in the containment with very precise pressure instruments; you measure the average temperature in the containment using a number, perhaps 20 to 30 RTDs, resistance temperature detectors, that are scattered through the containment.

A weighting factor is applied to those temperatures to give you an accurate representation of the average temperature, and you measure the humidity, because you need to be able to subtract the pressure of the water vapor out from the pressure of the gas, and with those measurements, you can calculate the mass of air in the containment.

MR. JONES: You're right. That was pretty simple.

No

MR. SMITH: She said "no."

Q. Is the answer "no"?

A. "No."

MR. SMITH: Did you say "no"?

THE WITNESS: Yes.

MR. SMITH: You said "no"?

THE WITNESS: "No."

Q. For my clarification, the answer is "no" to the question, or "no" you're not going to answer the question?

A. I answered the question "no."

Q. Your answer is "no" to the question, then?

A. Yes.

MR. HARRIS: You said OK to that?

MR. SULLIVAN: I can't wait to read the transcript.

Get to the Point

Q. Were there any traffic considerations involved in removing that existing bridge?

A. As far as traffic considerations, by removing the existing bridge, we have improved the roadway from the standpoint that the vertical curvature of the road we can flatten somewhat so we have better sight distances, especially considering we're coming into a decision zone for the motorist here of where we have better sight distances, so it is a flatter road profile.

THE COURT: Does that mean you took the hill out?

THE WITNESS: Exactly.

A Long Response to a Simple Question

Q. What about your clothing for $60 a month, do you spend $60 a month on clothes?

A. Again, that is an estimate of what I spend.

Q. Is that correct?

A. I believe so.

Q. And do you save any receipts for that?

A. I have some.

Q. They come to $60 a month?

A. This is an estimate.

Q. Did they come up to $60 a month?

A. This is an estimate of what I spend.

Q. Did they come up to $60 a month?

A. This is an estimate of what I spend and what I have figured out I spend on my clothes.

Q. Do your receipts come up to $60 a month for your clothes that you kept?

A. Again, this is an estimate of what I spend.

Q. Do the receipts that you've kept for your clothing expenses come up to $60 a month?

A. I do not have all my receipts, therefore it is not an exact number.

Q. So the answer is "no"?

A. I believe I've answered this question.

The $3 Answer

Q. Who is the tenant in that one?

A. The one that's rented?

Q. Yes, sir.

A. Well, it's a Japanese name, but he's a Mexican or an Indian. I'm not sure. I think he's a Mexican. He could be Indian. He works at the Indian hospital. I guess he's an Indian. I don't know what you're laughing about.

Q. It's just cost me about three bucks for you to answer that question and you didn't say anything.

A. Well, I don't know. I can't remember his name. I just got a check from him last night. I don't remember.

Q. I've got to pay for each line of this thing.

A. I'll make it shorter then. I don't know. Is that better?

Case Closed

Q. What do you mean when you say your file is closed?

A. Closed to you may mean differently, but to me it's closed. To you closed means closed, but it may mean open also. But to me it's closed, but I can go back and open it. So, don't look at it in saying because you say closed, closed means closed. No. As far as my books are concerned, closed is closed, but it's open. Anything is open that I do. Did you get that?

Q. OK.

"Since you've already been convicted by the media, why don't you just plead guilty and save the State the cost of a trial?"

Courts Interrupt Us

MR. LAVIN: My objection is I would prophylactically object to any question—

THE COURT: Prophylactically?

MR. LAVIN: I am not talking about preventing contraception, Judge. I am talking about preventing the line of questioning that would be outside the scope of—

THE COURT: Your prophylactic objection is premature.

MR. LAVIN: I will withdraw it.

Novel Objection

MR. SMITH: I object to that because — well, I'll object to that statement that Jim is lying as being something that I'll figure out later.

MR. BROWN: Going back to the question, I'll restate it. I must remember that objection. That's beautiful.

A Matter of Definition

Q. And as I understand it, the company's line of work includes nutrition for animals, humans and plants; correct?

MR. JONES: I want to object to the form of the question in that it separates humans from animals, and humans are animals.

MR. SMITH: Maybe the humans you know are animals.

Objectionable Objection

MR. GREEN: I can't believe that objection is being made quoting me by the person who objected to my making the objection when I made it.

Nonobjection Sustained

MR. BURGESS: For the record, I'm going to object to this line of questioning; however, I'm not going to actually object.

THE COURT: I sustain your nonobjection.

The Sounds of Silence

MR. FRANKLIN: I think he said—

MR. JONES: I heard his answer.

MR. FRANKLIN: Please don't interrupt me.

MR. JONES: Is it an objection, Mr. Franklin?

MR. FRANKLIN: Mr. Jones, if you would not interrupt me and you would listen to what I'm saying, then your question as to what it is would be answered.

MR. JONES: Fine.

MR. FRANKLIN: Let me finish.

MR. JONES: I thought you were finished.

MR. FRANKLIN: When I'm done it's easy to tell. I stop talking and there's no more noise coming from my mouth.

Invasion of Privacy

Q. Were you sterile at the time of delivery? Were you sterily gloved and gowned?

MR. JOHNSON: I'll object to the question as being compound.

MS. MCDONALD: And personal.

Doleful Disease

MR. DOE: We continue to object to the admission of Respondent's Exhibit 21 for identification for lack of foundation and because it is a document that has a severe double hearsay problem.

HEARING OFFICER: I hope I never catch that.

Fashion Statement

MR. WOLFE: Don't try to buffalo him and intimidate him by telling him what's going to happen at trial. That's what I object to.

MR. HASKINS: Any man that can wear those suspenders and that tie cannot be intimidated.

Words With Little Meaning

Q. Isn't it true that at one time, perhaps before you wrote this report, they were paid by the government, but after an instance in Brooklyn, where a malpractice case was brought against one of the Service Corps physicians, that the regulations were changed because an enterprising attorney decided to sue the federal government under the Tort Claims Act, and the public Health Service didn't want to be liable for the city anymore, therefore they changed the terms of all NHSC placements so that those doctors became employees of the health center?

MR. JONES: I object.

THE COURT: That was a remarkable question. Unparalleled in complexity. Unbelievable.

MR. BLACK: Are you suggesting I rephrase it?

THE COURT: I think you better.

Agreeable Witness

Q. I'm not saying that I can rephrase it, but I will try to. I will try to rephrase it in a way that you can understand it. And likewise, may we agree that if you don't tell me that you do not understand the question, that you do in fact do, that we can understand that if you don't tell me, when I ask the question, that it's not understood, that you have understood it?

MR. JONES: I object to the form of the question.

Q. Can we agree to that?

A. Yes.

Thinking of Horsing Around

Q. Ms. Davidson, can you indicate what time you heard these noises?

A. I thought it was approximately 7:30 as I didn't have a clock in the bedroom, and I got up and looked out at the horses and they were both standing there looking toward the road, sort of looking like something was going on.

MR. KINAR: Objection. I'm wondering, your Honor, if perhaps the witness could be cautioned not to speculate what might have been going on in the minds of the livestock?

THE COURT: I think you made your point.

Are You Sure?

Q. OK. On the first page, the original tape, how many is on there?

A. None.

Q. None?

A. None.

Q. None?

MR. BOYER: I'm going to object. Your Honor, I think that's been asked and answered.

A Clear Stipulation

MR. LIBOTT: Counsel, if you have no objection, I would like to stipulate and I think that we can save a lot of lawyer talking if we agree that simply a reference to those letters or to that oral agreement, an agreement, or alleged agreement did not waive our position that the agreement does not consist of an agreement, and that the letters nor other conversation consisted of the agreement, nor your position that they do, and therefore we don't have to keep saying "alleged" and "averred" and all those sorts of things.

Is that all right with everybody?

MR. FOLINSKY: No problem with me.

MR. BRIDGES: No objection.

Oh, Wilbur

Q. Do you know of any racetracks in California where they use means other than human beings on the starting gate to determine when to open the gate?

MR. MANUWAL: I'm going to interpose an objection. That's vague and ambiguous and unintelligible. What do you mean by "means other than human beings"? For instance, other horses?

Adding His Two Cents' Worth

Q. So you're telling the Court that as you sit here today you gross $750.77 per week, is that right?

A. Correct.

Q. And if we can trust my calculator—

MR. RAUCH: Stipulate to the reliability of the calculator, object to the competency of the operator. I withdraw that.

Grammatical Objections

Q. So actually you got along very good with Mr. Stitely; is that right?

A. Yes.

MR. IPSEN: Objection, your Honor. I think that would be, she got along well with Mr. Stitely.

THE COURT: Well, is that a legal objection? What are the grounds?

MR. IPSEN: Actually, I can't articulate the grounds, your Honor.

THE COURT: Mr. Blum, your question is grammatically inadequate but legally sufficient.

Something to Whet the Palate

Q. What did she do when she got there?

A. She removed a black bottle of grand mariner—

THE COURT: It's Grand Marnier.

THE WITNESS: OK, Grand Marnier. I won't argue with the Court on that.

Thanks for Telling Me
MR. JONES: I am going to interpose a late objection that this line of questioning is irrelevant and not likely to lead to the discovery of relevant evidence.

MR. SMITH: Jeez, I better go on to something else then.

And Furthermore ...
MR. CONN: I'm going to object to that question. It's repetitious, redundant, it's been asked and answered, it's without any foundation, calling for a conclusion, calling for conjecture and speculation, irrelevant and immaterial, and boring.

Hardly
Q. Did the defendant have an erection?

THE DEFENSE: Objection. Calls for expert medical opinion.

THE COURT: I don't think so.

Amen

Q. When he went, had you gone and had she, if she wanted to and were able, for the time being excluding all the restraints on her not to, gone also, would he have brought you, meaning you and she, with him to the station?

MR. BROOKS: Objection. That question should be taken out and shot.

"Isn't the right to bare arms in the Constitution?"

Credit Where Credit Is Due

Q. This business about an erection, was that brought up to you or was that something you brought up?

A. I never brought it up. The only time I ever brought it up is when I questioned why it was in that report.

Really Cooperating

Q. Will you tell us, did you personally show the books or did somebody else that was working for you?

A. Our bookkeeper, Mrs. Smith, had cooperated with their representatives, which was, as I understand, an accountant. In fact she spent several nights with the accountant just trying to be cooperative.

Localized Area

Q. Mr. Crawford, since August 8, have you received any medical care or treatment?

A. Yes.

Q. For what condition?

A. I had a dog bite I was treated for.

Q. When did it occur?

A. I believe that was either in the winter of '83 or spring of '84.

Q. And where was the bite received?

A. On Route 42.

Q. No, what portion of the body?

A. Leg.

One Step Closer to Broadway

Q. The name of the paper is "The Immunohistochemical Localization and Distribution of Cyclic Nucleotides in the Rat's Mandibular Condyle in Response to an Induced Occlusal Change"?

A. Correct.

Q. Did I pronounce that right?

A. Beautiful.

Q. What part did you have to play in that paper?

A. I was the rat.

An Eye-Opening Response

Q. Do you wear a two-piece bathing suit now that you have a scar?

A. I don't wear a bathing suit at all now.

Q. That can be taken two ways.

Cutting to the Heart of the Matter

Q. Did you also do the cleaning at your daughter's house?

A. Not too often. My daughter would take care of those things.

Q. You do most of the cooking.

A. Yes.

Q. And did you do most of the laundry before this incident?

A. No. I used the washing machine.

Simplicity at its Best

Q. Do you remember what shoes you were wearing?

A. You mean the day I fell down?

Q. Yes.

A. The same shoes I'm wearing.

Q. What do you call those shoes? Are they flats or how would you describe them?

A. I'd describe them as "these shoes."

Undressed for Success

Q. Now, from your knowledge, sir, why did you tie up there on October 30, 1983?

A. Well, the owner of the boat tied it up because he was going to make some repairs on it.

Q. At that time was there any agreement between you and the captain or you and the owner about when you would go out again?

A. No. No, there wasn't. I just got my clothes off and started looking for another boat.

Barely Enough

Q. How many police officers?

A. Well, at the time at least 20 police officers at the scene of the crime.

Q. At least 20 police officers?

A. Including unclothed.

Dressed for Success

Q. At the time when you went in to talk to her about the job, were you wearing anything?

A. Yes, I had a brace on.

Interesting Exercise

Q. Where do you do aerobics?

A. At home.

Q. Was this on a regular basis?

A. Yes, three times a week, before I was pregnant three times a week.

Spell it, Please

Q. Where do you live?

A. LaPosta Trailer Court.

THE COURT: How do you spell that trailer court?

THE WITNESS: T-r-a-i-l-e-r C-o-u-r-t.

Variation on the Theme

Q. Have you ever beaten your wife?

A. No. I might have slapped her around a little, but I never beat her.

I Witness News

Q. Is this just something you have heard along the way or something you know of your own knowledge?

A. Something I know of my own knowledge.

Q. How do you know it?

A. I have seen it, witnessed it on television.

Clarifying for the Client

Q. How often do you wear the brace?

A. Maybe twice a week.

Q. Do you wear it to work?

A. Yes. I'm the foreman. I don't have to work.

MR. CONN: You mean you don't have to work like the laborers do.

THE WITNESS: Yes.

Blind Justice

DEFENSE ATTORNEY: There is nothing else I can say, other than to ask for a blindfold and a cigarette.

THE COURT: I can lend you the blindfold, but there's no smoking in here.

Grammatical Objections

MR. HOLMES: How do you plead to Count I, violation of Section 288(a) of the Penal Code, an act with a lewd minor?

THE DEFENDANT: Guilty.

THE COURT: Lewd conduct with a minor.

MR. HOLMES: Pardon me. How do you plead?

THE DEFENDANT: Guilty.

A Simple "No" Might Have Been Better

Q. Have you ever been qualified as an expert in any court to give testimony regarding the facts of wearing or not wearing a seat belt subsequent to 1989?

A. Never as a specific focus of an issue have I ever been qualified to give an opinion.

Knowing When to Keep Your Mouth Shut

THE COURT: Do you give up the right to have a preliminary hearing at this time and agree that this matter goes to the Supreme Court on the charge that's been filed against you which is an attempted second degree auto burglary?

THE DEFENDANT: It is not an attempt.

THE COURT: Well, that's what they charged you with.

MR. TURNER: He meant it was just an auto tampering, by the way.

I Swear

THE CLERK: Do you solemnly swear the testimony you're about to give in this matter will be the truth, the whole truth and nothing but the truth, so help you God?

THE WITNESS: May he strike me down if it ain't.

One Look Should Tell

THE COURT: The problem I have is in the past he's had this drug abuse problem and has quit in the past and then gone right back to drug use again. So what is this, just another interim period where he's going to go back to drug use once he is out of custody?

MR. SIMON: I don't have a crystal ball, your Honor. I don't know what steps he took in the past as compared to the steps he's taking now. And as the Court's aware, and I think we've discussed, a person has to bottom out. I don't know if this is the defendant's bottom. Maybe it is, maybe it isn't.

The Court Jester

MS. SMITH: If Mr. Johnson is suggesting that only he can raise that, I have never heard of that and would be real excited to hear some authority from him on that.

MR. JOHNSON: Your Honor, I'm always happy to excite Ms. Smith, so I will look up the authority.

THE COURT: Well, I'm sure you will. I'm sure you will both enjoy it.

Reason Enough

MILITARY JUDGE: Any suggestions of what prevented this from being a murder trial instead of an attempted murder trial?

A. The victim lived.

The I-Am-A-Sidewalk Syndrome

Q. Do you know what your medical condition is diagnosed as?

A. Yes, I do.

Q. What is that?

A. People walking on me.

Thirty-Second Employment

A. Oh, I had another job in there, too.

Q. Which one was that?

A. I filled in while someone had a heart attack.

Trucking Loaded

(The deponent was being questioned about his truck-driving business.)

Q. Can you come home loaded? Excuse me; I didn't mean that the way it sounded.

Don't Point at Loaded People

Q. Did you ever see him point guns at people that were loaded and things like that prior to this incident?

A. Yes.

Don't Ride on the Handlebars

Q. Where were you on the bike at that time?

A. On the seat.

Q. I mean where in the street?

Heavy Water

Q. Is it also true that water is heavy when it's standing on a building?

A. It's not any heavier than at any other time.

How Many Miles Does it Get per Battery?

Q. The Mercedes that has been scratched that you claim was scratched by the flashlight that you were driving on that night?

A. Right.

MR. LAWRENCE: I think the court reporter has a problem with your question.

Witness Tells Counsel Where to Go

Q. You told me you know how to get there. Tell me how to get there.

A. You take a bus and you cross the street and you get into the office.

Why Would I Cheat?

Q. Did you receive money in exchange for what you sold him?

A. Yes.

Q. How much money did you get?

A. $25.

Q. All right. And how much did you sell him?

A. $25 worth.

Let George Do It

Q. There's a name on here, George R-e-s-i-n-d-a-s. Do you know how to pronounce his name, so I won't butcher it?

A. George.

Lively Location

Q. Where were you when you fell two years ago?

A. In a hurry.

Clip, Clop, to the Beauty Shop
Q. Just briefly tell me what happened in the accident.

A. Well, briefly, what happened, a lady was going to the beauty shop, and I was between her and the beauty shop, and she took me with her.

Ultimate Rejection
Q. If someone is not hired as an employee, are they kept for some period of time and then ultimately destroyed?

Child Labor
Q. And how much did the father of the child's employer make?

If We Scratch it, Can We Strike it Too?
Q. Yes, I understand. But — scratch my "but."

"X" Marks the Spot

Q. Please put an "X" where you fell.

A. On my behind?

Q. No, I meant on the exhibit.

Being Specific

Q. Mrs. Rand, once again, please pay close attention to the question and only answer the question. Do you understand?

A. Yes, I understand.

Q. At the time of the impact, can you estimate how many feet you were pushed back?

A. Yes.

Q. Well, how many?

A. Both.

Q. What?

A. Two. This one and this one (indicating).

Sorry, Judge

MR. ALLENBY: The reason we selected the 12 of you to hear this matter is because we wanted people to hear it who had common sense. Otherwise, we'd just have the judge hear this case.

Reword That, Please

Q. You testified that the first sentence was not limited to in-house training programs?

A. That's correct.

Q. It relates also to outhouse — or should I say outside training programs; correct?

A. Absolutely, counselor.

Language Barriers

Q. Sir, you have been handed a document that has been marked 310. Is this in the Greek language, sir?

A. This is Greek language, yes.

Q. Would you please read to us, sir, what this says?

A. Opos htehsini tilofoniki—

Q. Let me rephrase the question.

A. You would like it translated?

Derogatory Testimony

Q. Did you review any records before you came here?

A. I discussed with my attorney the derogatories.

Q. Interrogatories?

A. Interrogatories. Yes, sir.

Look Out

Q. When you're sitting there, you have your vehicle sitting on the drive into the garage and you look out the left side of your vehicle with the vehicle facing in, are you then looking through a series of rose bushes followed by a hedge?

A. I'm looking through the window of the car.

Really?

Q. Now, fourth-grade reading level, how low is that?
A. Fourth grade.

Daffynition

Q. Please review this document. Do you know what a fax is?

A. Yeah, I do, man. It's when you tell the truth, man, tell it like it is. That is what the facts is.

No Way to Treat a Customer

Q. Was that a loader that was used on farmlands where you had stored manure?

A. Yes, sir.

Q. And you were loading trucks there with that loader—

A. Yes, sir.

Q. —which was being spread on those customers of yours?

A. That is correct.

Deposition Definitions

Q. Have you ever had your deposition taken before today?

A. Is this a deposition?

Q. A deposition is like in front of a court reporter. Have you ever had an instance where you were under the court reporter and you were encouraged to tell the truth?

A. Never.

Pocket-Sized Pickup

Q. Did either of the defendants have any documents or other items on their persons that attracted your attention?

A. Yes. George had the registration that belonged to the red pickup in his pocket.

But My Feet Reach the Floor

Q. Have you had training and experience with small arms?
A. Yes, I have. I've grown up with small arms all my life.

Something New on the Menu

Q. Do you serve the fruits and the salads or do you only prepare them?

A. Well, since most of these fruits are canned, we have to prepare them and we have to open the cans and then prepare them in small little cups for each individual.

Q. Do you actually serve the children after you take them out of the cans?

The Fabric of His Defense

A. I told my attorney I would take that polyester test to show I wasn't lying, but no one every gave me one.

Memory Is a Fragile Thing

Q. I want to know what you recall feeling physically.

A. I can't remember what I recall.

Guilty Until Proven Innocent

Q. Do you think you can be a fair and impartial juror in this trial?

A. Sure.

Q. Do you know the defendant?

A. Yeah.

Q. How well do you know him?

A. Well, not too well; just to speak to him and stuff.

Q. When was the last time you saw the defendant before this date?

A. Let's see. Oh, yeah. It was the day he stole the money.

Teletraveling
A. They invited us to come for Easter to Austin by phone.

Victimless Crime
THE COURT: Anyone victims of a crime to yourself or your property?

JUROR: Yes, sir. We were broken into several times maybe about five or six years ago, but the victims were not found.

Slipping Through the Cracks
Q. Could you briefly go over with me your educational background, the extent of your education?

A. I went to high school for 12 years.

"Bambi"

A. The only thing I recall is looking out the window and down the hillside and noticing some deer — mother deer and the little babies — walking around.

Q. Grazing?

A. Yes.

Q. On the hillside?

A. Yes.

THE COURT: You didn't know at the time they were DEA agents, I guess?

THE WITNESS: I didn't, no.

Not a Transsexual, Then?

Q. Can you describe the person you saw standing outside the van? Was he white, black, man, woman?

A. It must have been something like in between?

Q. I assume in between black and white?

A. Yes.

SPF 45?

Q. What prompted you to call her?

A. She called me, to begin with. This was on a tangenital issue.

The Afterlife

Q. You knew the estate had been probated in Arizona?

A. I am not sure what "probate" means.

Q. When someone dies, you are aware what happens; aren't you?

A. I still don't understand, sir.

Q. When someone dies, it is where they live.

About Leading Three Lives — and Canine Lives

Q. In the Florida case, was it also marked in evidence that your wife had committed suicide several times down there?

A. Yes, ma'am.

Q. And how many times had she committed suicide while in Florida?

A. Three different times I know of.

Cluck, Cluck

Q. Where you do work?

A. 3-D Poultry Loading.

Q. And what are your duties there?

A. Catch chickens.

Q. What's your job title?

A. Well, I guess I'm a chicken catcher.

Q. I had to ask.

"Please, Mother, not yet!"

What Does That Make Us?

Q. Tell us how you know him.

A. Robert's mother is my sister's — my mother's sister's husband's sister. In other words, his mother — his mother's brother is married to my aunt.

MR. CORTS: I don't want to know any more than that.

Having Dinner at the Stork Club, Maybe?

Q. Were you just visiting Grand Junction, Tennessee, at the time you were born?

She's Normal

Q. I take it from what you have told me that prior to 1981 she was not irritable or forgetful?

A. She forgot things, yes, but everybody forgets things.

Q. How about being irritable?

A. Well, whenever the kids were small, she was irritable, yes.

My Good Friend What's-His-Name

Q. What is Mr. Lang's first name?

A. We're real close cousins. Ed. No, that's not it. That's his older brother. Mary Ann is his wife's name, if that helps.

Since He Conceived of the Possibility

(From voir dire of a potential juror whose father happened to be the public defender:)

MR. BRITTON: Mrs. Stoffle, I think it's important to tell you that I know your father, too, and have known him for quite some time. These discussions that you had with your father—

MRS. STOFFLE: Yes.

MR. BRITTON: He's been your father for a long time?

MRS. STOFFLE: Yes.

MR. BRITTON: So, has he — well, that's true isn't it? In my own defense, we don't take anything for granted.

When You Wish Upon a Star

Q. You're telling this Court that you never had sexual intercourse with this gentleman, but yet you claim that he is the father of your five-year-old child?

A. That's right.

Q. Was this another star-in-the-east situation?

A. I don't know how it happened.

Everybody Needs Them

Q. You can't play with the grandchildren anymore?

A. I can read them a story or something like that. But so far as anything that takes like throwing a ball with my hand or anything like that, I can't do.

Q. Can you hug them?

A. They're boys. They don't need to be hugged much.

Family Tree Needs Pruning

Q. What is the relationship?

A. She's my aunt.

Q. Who's brother or sister to whom here?

A. My mother is his brother — is her — my mother is — what is it? By marriage, I guess you would say. My mother is her brother — is his brother by marriage, so she's just an aunt.

That's What I Thought You Asked

Q. Now, Mr. Stern. Your mother, Helen Stern, lives here in Madera. You know her pretty well?

A. Who?

Q. Your mother.

A. In what area?

Q. Your mom.

A. My mom is Helen Stern.

Q. Helen Stern?

A. Yes.

Q. Do you know her pretty well?

A. She raised me.

Unusual Questions

Q. Do you have any children?
A. Yes, sir, I have three.
Q. Are they boys, girls or what?

Searching for the Obvious

Q. And who owned the car?
A. My mom and dad.
Q. And they're you're parents?
A. Yeah.

Pray Tell

Q. List the last names of the relatives either on your husband's side or on your side.

A. On either side?

Q. Yes, ma'am.

A. Every relative?

Q. Their last names. What families are you related to in that area?

A. Well, I have uncles.

Q. What are their names?

A. Varela, Quintann — oh, shoot. I have to go through four families? My Mom's side, my Dad's side?

Q. Just the same. Who are you related to?

A. Jesus Christ!

Q. We're all related to him.

Alleged Offspring

A. I'm not even sure of the number. It was a number of boys involved. In fact, allegedly even one of them was the son of a board member. Not allegedly was a son; allegedly a son was involved. He was really the son.

Thanks for Clarifying

Q. Do you know who Joe Dickerson Jr. is?

A. Yes, I do.

Q. Do you know who Joe Dickerson Sr. is?

A. Yes. And now that you mention junior and senior I don't know which is the one I know the best.

Q. One's older, one's younger.

House Slippers

Q. All right. So the day they came to your mother's house you saw Johnny talking to Chino; is that correct?

A. No. When I got there, I was at my sister's home. They were waiting for me at the house, so I came from my sister's house and they left my mother's house to my sister's house, but I was already coming to my mother's house, so they got to my sister's house, and they called over at the house, and I was there at my mother's house. They came back.

Relatively Speaking

THE JUROR: Judge, I don't know if this is relevant or not, but my husband's cousin's husband's ex-wife is pregnant by the defendant, or supposed to be.

Canine Patrol

THE COURT: Do you have any friends or relatives in law enforcement?

THE WITNESS: No, in law enforcement. Would you consider an animal control supervisor of Eagle County law enforcement?

THE COURT: I suppose if they arrested your dog you would.

The Natural Order

Q. Approximately how old was his father?

A. His father was older than he was.

Q. Well, that's always good.

A Truer Word

Q. Do you know if there's a history of heart trouble in your family?

A. Well, when we all die, we gonna have heart trouble.

I Just Call Him What's His Name

Q. What is your brother-in-law's name?

A. Borofkin.

Q. What's his first name?

A. I can't remember.

Q. He's been your brother-in-law for 45 years, and you can't remember his first name?

A. No, I tell you I'm too excited. (Rising from the witness chair and pointing to Mr. Borofkin:) Nathan, for God's sake, tell them your first name!

My Memory's Good, But ...

Q. When you were born, do you recall any medical history that would show you have any congenital defects?

A. I can't recall from then.

What a Difference a Comma Makes

Q. Did he ever discuss the fact that he had a daughter, with you?

How Could You Forget?

Q. How old is your son, the one living with you?

A. Thirty-eight or 35, I can't remember which.

Q. How long has he lived with you?

A. Forty-five years.

"Who needs soap operas, when you have the real thing?"

New Classification
Q. What is your marital status?
A. Right now it's not too good.

Cause and Effect?
Q. What's your first recollection at the Royal Columbian Hospital?
A. Waking up and seeing my girlfriend there and then throwing up.

The Case of the Paranormal Spouse
Q. Mr. Jones, do you believe in alien forces?
A. You mean other than my wife?

Novel Defense

Q. It is true what the petitioner says, that you're living with another man?

A. It's true.

Q. Do you know that that's adultery, a crime in New York state?

A. But I'm moving to New Jersey.

Make Yourself at Home

Q. Sir, have you and your wife cohabitated since March 6, 1975?

A. Only here in court on April 3.

"What Ever Happened To Baby Jane?"

Q. When was the next occasion that you had difficulty with your wife?

A. April 27, I believe it was, when she backed over me with the automobile.

Just Compensation

Q. And for your daughter's helping you with your paper route, you didn't pay them by check, you just paid them in cash?

A. Yes, sir.

Q. All right. And your husband also helped you with your paper route. Did you pay him also?

A. Hey, I pay him all the time.

Two-for-One Sale

Q. Recently you sold your home along with your wife; is that correct?

The Marrying Kind

Q. With respect to your previous marriages, those were all in and around Silsbee?

A. No. One in Brooklyn, Texas; one in Sour Lake; one in Louisiana. And one time I was drunk; I don't know where that was at. My daughter typed up the divorce papers, and I filed them myself, and the judge gave me a divorce, told me I was a lucky scamp. And then this woman here is here to stay, so I ain't got that problem no more.

Q. That divorce was up in Silsbee?

A. Yes.

Q. And the one before was somebody that you knew you were married to?

A. I have to admit, now, when I was a young buck I was about half crazy. There was two things I liked to do then, is run hot cars and fool with women.

Understandable Confusion

Q. And who else lives in the house beside you and Sam Albright?

A. No one but my dog Jasper.

Q. Is he married?

A. Jasper?

Q. Mr. Albright?

A. No, he is divorced.

Lasting Love

Q. Did you leave the company on good terms?

A. Yes, I did.

Q. Why did you leave?

A. Fell in love and wanted to move to the mountains.

Q. Fell in love with a girl or the mountains?

A. Both. The mountains are still there.

Q. Little more dependable?

A. I have a feeling they'll be around a lot longer, too.

Definition of Prolific

Q. How many children do you have?

A. What do you mean?

Q. Did you understand my question?

A. Yeah, but you don't understand mine.

Q. I said, how many children do you have?

A. Twenty-seven.

Q. OK.

A. You should ask me what you mean. You didn't say by my wife. You said how many children did I have.

Q. And you've got nine by your wife?

A. That's right.

Q. Are there 18 by any prior wives?

A. Well, I got two kids by my first wife.

Q. And the others, you were not married to the mothers?

A. That's right.

Pet Names
Q. So, besides your wife and children, do you have any other animals or pets?

Wait Till We Get Home!
Q. When did you and your wife get married? Give me a year? A decade?

A. What do I win?

Q. Marital bliss for the next 10 minutes.

A. April 12 or March?

Q. Just tell me what year.

A. We got married in '67.

THE WITNESS'S WIFE: '65.

THE WITNESS: '65. That's right. I had that new car. I should have remembered that.

Secret of Success

Q. What would you do with your time off work? Would you go home and just read, or can you give me an idea?

A. I would leave work at 5:30, quarter to 6 or so, and I would go home.

Q. And you would usually spend your time home then in the evening?

A. That's why I've been married 42 years.

Singular Distinction

Q. What did he say?

A. About that? All the way back he — I've never been called so many names.

Q. You're not married, I take it.

That's the Usual Sequence

Q. Are you married?

A. I'm divorced.

Q. So you were married at one point in time?

Finding Good in all Things

Q. Indicating that your left ear gives you problems?

A. It doesn't give me problems. I just can't hear out of it. But that's OK. I can hear good out of this ear. I lay on my good ear when I know I have to listen to my wife.

That State of Marriage

Q. How many states have you lived in?

A. Well, you should ask me how many states I haven't lived in?

Q. All right. Which states haven't you lived in?

A. Alaska and Hawaii.

Q. Why have you lived in so many states?

A. Well, every time I get a divorce, I move.

Not-Too-Brief Encounter
Q. Where was the marriage encounter?
A. At St. Francis in San Juan Bautista.
Q. How long did that retreat last?
A. Too long.

Cleaning Up Their Act
Q. What did your husband say, if anything, when he came into the kitchen?
A. He said, "You dirty bitch, I'm going to break your neck."
Q. What did you say?
A. Nothing.
Q. Then what happened?
A. I threw the Drano in his face.

Another Word for Divorce
Q. Have you always lived in Beaumont since you came off the farm?
A. No, I lived in Orange before I married and demarried.

Evasive Answer

Q. Prior to your wife's surgery, how often were you having sexual relations?

A. Any time I could get a hold of her.

Be My Baby

A. I personally would not want that anesthesiologist anesthetizing my wife for a C-section.

Q. Even if your baby, your own personal baby, was in the uterus?

A. I hope it's my baby in my wife's uterus.

Hey, Watch Your Language!

Q. Did you cohabitate with this lady at all during the year of 1975?

A. I never did that at all; she's a nice lady. And, your Honor, I wish you would tell this young man not to talk this way about her.

THE COURT: Counsel, I don't believe he understands the word cohabitate.

Q. Did you live with or reside in the same house with her during 1975?

A. Well, yes, I did that, but we never did what you are trying to say.

It Ought to Be a Crime

Q. Have you had any business with the District Attorney's office?

A. Other than my divorce, this is the only thing I've been to court for.

Q. That's not a crime. I can testify to that. So can the judge.

A. I don't know. When I looked at the settlement, I damn sure thought it was a crime.

That's the Way it Is

Q. How long have you been married to Theresa?

A. Thirty-two years.

Q. OK. Were you ever married before?

A. I am Italian. I am Catholic. Born once, die once, you marry once. I am also a right-wing Republican, so don't ask me any dumb questions.

Q. Do you have any children?

A. Yes. They are both accidents.

A Pattern Develops

Q. You were married twice, right?

A. Married three times.

Q. Three times. How did the marriages end?

A. Ended up with me being single.

The Record Speaks

THE COURT: Can we continue this case to this afternoon?

MS. SMITH: Judge, I will not be here this afternoon or the rest of the week.

THE COURT: Or the rest of the week?

MS. SMITH: I'm on my 15th anniversary.

MR. FIELDS: I would ask of what, your Honor.

MS. SMITH: Of a great marriage and sex life. How is that?

MR. FIELDS: I'd request a transcript.

Yours, Mine, But Not Ours

Q. How did that marriage end?

A. Real fast.

Q. Did it end from divorce?

A. Yeah.

Q. Do you have any kids from that marriage?

A. No. I didn't, but she did.

An Uncomfortable Subject

Q. Throughout your notes you mention, well a couple of times anyway, various gynecological problems she had. Do you remember that, sir? I'd refer you to your May 19, 1993, note.

A. Vaginal warts. Yes.

Q. And do you know from whom she got the warts?

A. Well, she blamed her husband.

Q. And how did that make her feel?

A. She was mad at him.

Q. Why was she mad at him?

A. Women usually don't like to get vaginal warts and are sort of mad at whom they feel gave it to them.

Mark the Calendar

Q. Could you describe to me if there's any effect on your marriage as a result of your foot?

A. What, all the sleepless nights and all the pain and all the bitching and aggravation that I gave this poor man over here? Yes, I'd say there's a little bit of an effect on my marriage, wouldn't you?

Q. Do you still behave in that manner towards your husband?

A. Only once a month.

Makes You Wonder, Doesn't It?

Q. Were you employed prior to working for the Naval Air Station in Fallon?

A. My ex-husband and I had a dairy in Fernley.

Q. And how long did you operate the dairy?

A. Three and a half years before he defected.

Q. You mean he died?

A. No, he defected. He went back to his second wife — I mean, his first wife. I was number three. He went back to his first wife.

235

Grounds for Marriage

Q. What happened to your right eye?

A. Got shot.

Q. What was that all about?

A. It was with my ex-wife

Q. She shot you in the face?

A. Right.

Q. I assume you got a divorce from her after that?

A. No.

Q. How long did you stay married?

A. About six months. We hadn't been married when this happened.

Q. Oh, you weren't married? She shot you and you got married afterwards?

A. Yes.

Planning Ahead

Q. When did you begin to plan your wedding?

A. Well, actually, I didn't plan my wedding; my mother did.

Q. Did you participate in your mother's planning of your wedding?

A. No. My family is Italian.

Q. When did your mother begin to plan your wedding?

A. When I was born.

Don't Tell Her Husband

Q. What is your name?

A. Ernestine McDowell.

Q. And what is your marital status?

A. Fair.

Interaction

Q. I take it that before this accident happened you lived with your brother-in-law and sister for about six months?

A. Yes.

Q. You got to know him quite well?

A. Yes.

Q. You saw him interact with your sister, and I believe they had one child?

A. I didn't see the actual interaction, but they did have one child.

Wrong Vowel

Q. What does your husband do?

A. He's a shingle sawyer at Honeymoon Bay, where we got married.

Q. And where is that?

A. Honeymoon Bay is right by the Sex Camp he was working at.

THE REPORTER: Did you say "Sex Camp"?

THE WITNESS: Six Camp. They're all numbered. Six Camp, Seven Camp.

MR. JOHNS: You've still got Honeymoon Bay on your mind, Mr. Reporter. You hear only what you want to hear.

Helpmate

Q. What were you expecting from your marriage that never occurred?

A. Well, somebody to help shoulder the burden of being married.

Settlement Trade-Off

Q. Did you tell your lawyer that your husband had offered you indignities?

A. He didn't offer me nothing; he just said I could have the furniture.

Where Ignorance Is Bliss

Q. Are you married?

A. No, I'm divorced.

Q. What did your husband do before you divorced him?

A. A lot of things that I didn't know about.

Father's Day

PROSPECTIVE JUROR: Judge, I would like to be excused from the jury because my wife is about to become pregnant.

COUNSEL: Judge, he doesn't mean his wife is about to become pregnant; he means she is about to deliver.

THE COURT: You are excused. In either event he should be present.

Constrictions

Q. Did you have your headlights on?

A. Yes, I did.

Q. Were you doing anything that was distracting: listening to the radio, talking, fooling around?

A. Nothing. That's one reason I was going home, she wouldn't let me fool around.

Now We're Getting Somewhere

Q. Did you ever stay all night with this man in New York?
A. I refuse to answer that question.
Q. Did you ever stay all night with this man in Chicago?
A. I refuse to answer that question.
Q. Did you every stay all night with this man in Miami?
A. No.

Has This Happened More Than Once?

Q. Isn't it true that on the night of June 11, in a prune orchard at such and such location, you had relations with Mr. Blank on the back of his motorcycle?

(There was a complete silence for about three minutes, then the wife replied.)

A. What was that date again?

Which Habits?

Q. And people aren't coming into your store to do their staple grocery shopping?

A. It depends on your definition of "staple grocery shopping."

Q. Your once-a-week trip to the grocery store to stock up on your milk and eggs and cheese and meat and vegetables.

Are you married?

A. Some people don't have those habits.

Medical Malpractice

"Actually, DNA means 'Don't Know Anything.'"

Double Entendre

Q. Do you consider sitting on the sofa with a female patient during therapy to be within the appropriate standard of care in the handling of a female patient?

MR. ARENZ: I assume "the handling of a female patient" is not intended to have a double entendre?

Layman's Language

Q. What was the diagnosis of the report?

A. Headaches and acute subluxation complex of the cervical spine associated with radiculitis, myositis and spasm of the cervical paravertebral musculature.

Q. In layman's terms, would you explain that for us, Doctor?

A. It was a neck strain.

New Medical Terms

Q. Is there a diagnosis or a name for this problem that he has?

A. Yeah. Crushed foot.

Q. There's no medical term for it?

A. Crush-tis foot-tis.

Q. Other than the fact that he complains of the pain, is there anything else that indicates the problem?

A. Yeah. I've been in there and looked at the crush-tis foot-tis with the eye-yis. Yeah.

The Latter Is Better

Q. What other health problems do you have?

A. My heart doesn't beat.

Q. OK.

A. It beats real fast.

Another Reason for Masks

Q. But the anesthesiologist did not assist you in the operation?

A. No.

Q. But merely monitored her unconscious condition and passed gas and that sort of thing, right?

A. True.

Thank You

Q. Dr. Drinival, would you state your complete name for the record, please.

A. Kethandapatti Gopalaswarmi Drinival. Will K.G. do?

MR. SEIBEL: I'll stipulate to that.

Explosive Example

(During an attempted-murder trial, defense counsel was caught looking through the file of the psychiatrist on the stand. Cross-examination resumed:)

Q. And in those instances when the silent attack (of isolated explosive disorder) occurs, is it a fact that the specific intent itself may be lacking or nonexistent?

A. Well, when I walked into the courtroom and saw you rifling through my papers after I had specifically asked you not to, I could have picked up a chair and struck you over the head with it.

Q. Did you feel like that, Doctor?

A. I did. And I could have at that point been diagnosed as having isolated explosive disorder because I generally don't behave that way.

I'd Change My Name
Q. Are you seeing a psychiatrist now?
A. Yes.
Q. What's the psychiatrist's name?
A. Dr. Kwak.

Those Modern Doctors
Q. Mrs. Lang, regarding Dr. Greene, did Richard ever go to him?
A. He accompanied me there. Dr. Greene is a gynecologist.
Q. But did he receive any treatment from Dr. Greene?
A. No.
MR. BONNELL: Let's hope not, Joe.
MR. LANE: I didn't know. A lot of these doctors do a lot of things these days.

Patient Lacks Motivation — and a Pulse

Q. I suppose once you reach that level where you are dead you are not motivated by anything, are you?

A. Well, I'm not sure about that. I'm not really a theologian. I'm only a psychiatrist.

By All Means

Q. Doctor, did you have any indication that Mr. Jones is suffering from a herniated disk? Is it your conclusion that he is suffering from a herniated disk?

A. Do you have it in mind that you are asking me a simple question?

Q. It seems simple to me, but perhaps it isn't.

A. You are asking me one of the most complex questions that any orthopedist could be asked, and I could hold forth for several hours on the particular question.

Q. Then, by all means, let me withdraw that question.

A Positive Outlook

MR. JONES: The County has been talking about my client suffering from a mental illness. Well, in my family, we don't suffer from mental illness; actually, we rather enjoy it.

One Flew Over the Cuckoo's Nest

Q. Can you describe what it was like to be at Metropolitan State Hospital?

A. Scary.

Q. Why do you say that?

A. Because there was all sorts of very deranged, crazy people. And then there were the patients, who were worse.

Hoping for a Short Response

Q. Doctor, give us a brief history of the multiple occasions you have seen him.

A. Paraphrase the Bible in 25 words of less.

Life Imitates Art

Q. Can you give us the benefit of your educational background, please?

A. The benefit of my educational background has afforded me to treat patients in our community and allowed me to enjoy a rewarding professional career.

Sure Cure

Q. Doctor, what treatment did you give this man?

A. I cleansed the wound, sutured it and put him in bed with a nurse.

Older Than What?

Q. Do you associate any of those pains that come and go with the natural aging process?

A. What is that?

Q. Getting older.

A. Do I get older?

Q. Any of those pains, do you figure they come from getting older?

A. I wouldn't know. I've never been older before.

Concentration

Q. Now, Mrs. Marsh, your complaint alleges that you have had problems with concentration since the accident. Does that condition continue today?

A. No, not really. I take a stool softener now.

Practicing Medicine

Q. Was oxygen administered to you after the accident?

A. Yes.

Q. And do you know why that was the case?

A. No, I don't know why. I think they just want to practice.

Witnesses Say the Darnedest Things

Q. Do you remember what Dr. Thomason told you?

A. Yeah. That I had a — what do you call it — dislocated jaw. And I don't know the words that they use for it, but he told me that if I didn't get it taken care of that I'm really going to have serious problems in the future — that I didn't have the money to put down for my spleen.

Q. I beg your pardon?

A. He wants to put a spleen in my mouth.

Q. Very untasty.

MR. THEOBALD: You mean a splint?

Q. Splint sounds better than spleen.

A. Yeah.

Look Into My Eyes

Q. And did you have a chance to look into the person's eyes while he was acting like this?

A. Yes.

Q. And did they have a glazed look to them?

A. You're asking me to be a doctor. I don't know.

Q. Nurse practitioner would be all right. You can't tell if his eyes were glazed?

A. Not really.

Q. The pupils, did they appear in sort of a large stare or—

A. You know, having not really looked in his eyes before, I couldn't tell you if they were any different than they've ever been.

Lost in Thought

Q. You told her that before the surgery?

A. I said we could probably save the toes, but I don't know about the foot.

(Later ...)

Q. Did you have any discussion that you recall after the surgery?

A. I believe I told them that he was probably going to lose the leg, but at least maybe we could get lucky and save the toes, but I didn't think so.

Building Credibility

Q. I want you to assume, Doctor, that on pages 20 and 21 that my client, your patient, testified in a credible and forthright manner, just for the purpose of this question.

Was There a Warning Label?

Q. What happened when you took the medicine the doctor had prescribed for you, Mrs. Adams?

A. Well, sir, it gave me vomiting and gonorrhea.

Bedside Humor

Q. Mr. Johnson, your report indicates that the patient was lying on her back when you arrived to first administer first aid; correct?

A. Yes.

Q. Do you know where her legs were at the time you first arrived to administer first aid?

A. I don't recall.

MR. JONES: Still attached to her body, I hope.

Two Ways to See Things

Q. Doctor, will you take a look at those X-rays and tell us something about the injury?

A. Let's see, which side am I testifying for?

What, His House Didn't Burn Down, Too?

Q. I had a list of them. Let me see. He gave you a history of acute bronchitis, hepatitis, ruptured disk, fractured coccyx, carpal tunnel, carpal release in 1987, pneumonia, hypertension, hiatal hernia, colitis, duodena ulcer, and then he had some cholecystitis followed by a cholecystectomy and prior rectal surgery.

Do you think that might have some effect on his depressive symptom?

New Math

A. I asked her to do some mental arithmetic, serial sevens.

Q. Serial sevens are basically you ask the patient to go seven, 14, 21, 29 and so forth?

THE COURT: Twenty-one and seven is 28, not 29.

MR. EVERS: I must be depressed, your Honor.

A Breakthrough Procedure

Q. Further, Dr. Bostick was aware that Dr. Wilkins planned to do surgery on Mr. Polk by way of correspondence; is that correct?

A Place of Mishealing

Q. What happened with Scottie after he had his foot broken at the hospital?

Do You Accept Visa?

Q. How are you being compensated, Doctor, for your work in conjunction with this case?

A. I hope you people are going to write checks.

Oh, He Gives Me a Pain

Q. Are there any other conditions or doctors that you have either suffered from or been treated by?

The Devil, You Say?

Q. Have you ever told a doctor that you heard the voice of God?

A. That I've heard the voice of God?

Q. Yes.

A. Oh, I told him. He asked me if I heard anything. He said you got a conscience that talked to you.

Q. Did you ever tell him you talked to the devil?

A. I'm sorry. I haven't met him yet.

A Quick Cut

Q. I'd like to get the names of any doctors you've seen since about 1985 or '86. For instance, the doctor who did your vasectomy. Do you recall his or her name?

A. Doctor Gordon.

Q. Goldman?

A. Gordon, like Flash Gordon.

Q. I don't know if I'd want a vasectomy done by someone named Flash.

I Think That Answers It

Q. Has the doctor told you that you have had any kind of forgetfulness associated with that injury?

A. I don't remember.

Asymptomatic

MR. JOHNSON: Doctor, would you describe what happens in an epileptic seizure? I might be having one right now, and I wouldn't even know it.

Get the Job Done

Q. So, if it says in your medical records that you have tried on a number of occasions to kill yourself, that's not true?

A. No, that's not true. If I tried to kill myself a number of times, I would have succeeded at least once.

Knowing When to Quit

Q. OK, and I presume, sir, that you would anticipate that this dying patient would at some point pass away? I mean, that's a fair assumption?

A. That is the nature of death.

Q. Exactly.

A. Yes.

Q. And at some point in time there would be no need to continue prescribing this Dilaudid for that person because they were dead?

A. An excellent reason to stop.

Anatomy 101

Q. You don't have a cervix, do you?

A. What's a cervix?

Q. Well, in Answers to Interrogatories it says your cervix was X-rayed. I assume that's an error?

A. What's a cervix?

Q. You don't have one.

MRS. MILLS: I think I do.

Score One for the Memory Department

Q. Did you ever tell any of the doctors you saw that you were having problems with your memory?

A. I don't remember.

Expensive, But Honest

Q. Doctor, does your hourly rate change from testimony at deposition or trial?

A. No.

Q. No change at all?

A. No; still outrageous.

Nonprescription Strength

THE COURT: What type of drug was involved?

THE WITNESS: It wasn't a methamphetamine. It was a noncontrolled laxative.

THE COURT: Sounds like you would be in more trouble.

A Personal Favorite

A. I think once I was asked to talk about SIADH or something for about 10 minutes.

Q. What is SIADH?

A. Secretion of inappropriate antidiuretic hormone.

Q. It's always been one of my personal favorites.

Voodoo Medicine

Q. And then you went to which doctor?

A. Not a witch doctor.

Q. Pardon?

A. Did you say a witch doctor?

Q. No. Which doctor, which one?

A Morbid Sense of Humor

Q. And, Doctor, in this instance, do you know whether the information contained in those first two sentences came from the patient?

A. I'd assume that it came from whoever was informing me what happened, the patient with — or maybe his wife came along. I have no memory.

Q. All right. If a patient—

MR. COOPER: Can we go off the video for a second?

MR. SMITH: Sure.

VIDEOTAPE OPERATOR: We're now going off the record.

MR. COOPER: There's this noise—

THE WITNESS: That is the fire alarm.

MR. COOPER: Oh, but we're safe in the Chairman's office, right?

THE WITNESS: You're correct. We have great need for organs today, though, so be careful going out there. Anybody may be pronounced brain dead at any point.

MR. SMITH: Is there a particular organ I should keep a hand over?

Slight Rearrangement

Q. So after the anesthesia, when you came out of it, what did you observe with respect to your scalp?

A. I didn't see my scalp the whole time I was in the hospital.

Q. It was covered?

A. Yes, bandaged.

Q. Then later on, when you first observed it, what did you see?

A. I had a skin graft. My whole buttocks and my leg were removed and put on the top of my head.

"What happened after you asked the bakery clerk if her buns had sesame seeds?"

Absence of Malice

Q. You mentioned you've had some absences. What causes the absences? Is that work-related?

A. No. One day a shelf fell on my foot at work.

The Head Bone's Connected to the Foot Bone

Q. How were you injured?

A. I was hit on the head with a rock, and it broke my foot.

That's the Worst Kind

Q. What kind of pain did you experience, Mr. Smith?

A. Just plain pain. The kind that hurts.

Barnyard Audiometry

Q. Doctor, what test did you then perform on the patient?

A. I proceeded to examine his ears. Then tested his pitch with a tuning fork.

Q. Doctor, could you please tell us the exact procedure you used to test his hearing with a pitchfork?

Why?

Q. Did you use protection when you were welding on your face?

A Long Fall

Q. Have you ever received any on-the-job injuries?

A. A tractor dropped a blade on my foot.

Q. How far did it fall?

A. All the way to my foot.

Witnesses Fall on Bums

Q. How did she obtain the sprained ankle?

A. She was jogging on a tramp.

Dr. Jekyll and Mr. Hyde

A. That's part of the reason I don't remember most everything that I don't remember. I was told it was attributed to the hit on the head by two neurologists.

Novel Research Technique

Q. Does your practice regarding testing depend upon what instructions you get from the attorney?

A. Partially on that, and also the extent to which tests are feasible. We might, for example, take other Mitsubishi pickups and ask for volunteers to be hit by them. We would probably learn something by doing tests of that sort, but it's difficult to conduct them. Volunteers are hard to come by.

A Question of Location

Q. Has the company made a thorough search, in your mind, for any other promissory notes?

A. Not in my mind.

Double-Jointed Witness

Q. What kind of test did they do?

A. They tied up my ankle in a knot to hold the blood, and then they injected me in the left foot with a needle.

Overeager

Q. On the 29th of March, 1982, did you have occasion to perform an autopsy on Jane C?

A. Yes.

MILITARY JUDGE: Not likely.

TRIAL COUNSEL: Pardon me, your Honor?

MILITARY JUDGE: I said it's not likely, as she is seated in the courtroom.

Ouch!

Q. Have you been involved in other accidents — fallen at home or at work or anything like that?

A. No, except one time when I was in grade school my brother sat on my foot.

MR. PALMER: If you saw his brother, you would know why that was a problem.

Q. Did you break your foot?

A. No, I didn't; he broke it.

He Went Too Far

Q. You have given strong testimony against my client. Isn't it true that you hate my client?

A. Yes.

Q. Why do you hate my client?

A. When I broke my foot, he kicked my crutches out from under me. He stole my tractor. He stole my wife. He molested my daughter. He burned down my house. And he shot my dog. And I'd had that dog a long time.

Feeling a Little Run Down

A. And I was just aching everywhere. They said that was normal, that by tomorrow I would probably feel like a Mack truck had run over me.

Q. Is that the way you feel?

A. Worse, like they decided to go into reverse as well.

What's the Question?

Q. How were you feeling when you stopped seeing Dr. Nathan in your neck?

What's for Lunch?

Q. Can you describe her daily activities?

A. It's from bed to wheelchair to bed. Sometimes we nap together after lunch.

Q. Can she walk?

A. No, no, can't even stand up.

Q. Can she eat herself?

A. Yes.

Enlightening Testimony

Q. Would you please tell the Court what a "positive chandelier sign" is?

A. Well, that's when you manipulate the uterus with the patient lying on the table, and it causes such discomfort that they want to grab the chandelier if you have one in your office.

Anatomy 101

Q. When you looked at it, when your son was on the gurney at the hospital, what, if anything, did you see?

A. I seen a black puncture mark right below, I guess you call it, the uterus of the eye.

A Bee Line to Court

THE COURT: Do you have a coat, Mr. Jones?

MR. JONES: Your Honor, I was stung twice in the mouth by a yellow jacket a bit ago, and lost my coat. I don't know where it is, I am kind of getting my wits back.

THE COURT: You were being pursued by a yellow jacket and lost your coat in the process?

MR. JONES: I was drinking orange juice.

THE COURT: Are you all right now?

MR. JONES: I am kind of coming out of it. I had something to eat and took an antihistamine.

THE COURT: Are you allergic to a yellow jacket sting?

MR. JONES: No more than normal. I had a paralysis in my mouth. I was kind of confused, and I really don't know where I left my jacket.

THE COURT: Let's take up the motion to continue first.

MR. JONES: I still don't feel entirely comfortable, Judge. I swallowed the yellow jacket and he got me twice on the tongue. I didn't know what it was. He paid with his life.

EARLY COURT REPORTER

Amen (Hick!)

Q. Had to ever heard of this Normandy Company before?

A. No, sir.

Q. Have you spoken with anyone from that—

A. No, sir.

Q. —company?

A. No, sir.

Q. Do you know if Mr. Derer has spoken with anyone—

A. No, sir.

Q. —from that company? If you'd just let me finish the question. You wouldn't believe how bad it looks on this transcript, and it also drives court reporters to drink.

Like a Breath of Fresh Air

Q. Mr. Smith, let me suggest something to you that will make me real popular with my court reporter. Breathing would be appropriate in between some of these sentences, to allow her a chance to take down what you're saying, OK?

A. OK.

How Reporters Get Whiplash

Q. I'm just trying to get a feel for any litigation that your family—

A. Not that I know of, no.

Q. —has been involved in.

A. None.

Q. Let me tell you one other thing. We'll go a lot faster—

A. OK.

Q. —if you'll let me finish my question before you—

A. OK.

Q. —say anything, so he won't have to be—

A. I'm sorry.

Q. —writing us both at the same time.

A. OK.

Knock, Knock

Q. Have you ever been involved in any other motor vehicle accident?

A. Never in my life.

(The witness knocked on his head.)

Knock on wood.

MR. SMITH: The reporter didn't get that.

THE WITNESS: Put down knock knock knock.

Anyone Can Be a Magician

DEFENSE: You say you are a magician. Who do—

PROSPECTIVE JUROR: I was a magician on the Love Boat.

THE COURT: Sir, I'm going to have to ask you to quit cutting off the attorneys or you are going to see my reporter disappear.

Tooling Around

THE COURT: Sir, wait a minute. You keep cutting off the attorneys when—

THE WITNESS: I'm sorry.

THE COURT: —they ask you—

THE WITNESS: I'll be more careful.

THE COURT: —a question. What do you do for a living?

THE WITNESS: I install water heaters.

THE COURT: Do you use tools?

THE WITNESS: Yes.

THE COURT: How would you like it if someone stood behind you, and every time you started to turn a screw or something they yanked your tool out of—

THE WITNESS: I see. I'm sorry. I'm a little nervous.

THE COURT: —your hand? That's what you are doing. You keep yanking the words away from the reporter every time she starts to write. Do you think you can wait until—

THE WITNESS: Yes, I'm sorry.

And With Good Cause

MR. SMITH: Let me just say one thing for the court reporter's peace of mind. You let him finish his comment, even if you know what he's saying, and then he'll let you finish yours. Otherwise the record will be a mess and she'll physically assault both of you.

Endangered Species

(The prosecutor was handling a shotgun that had been marked as evidence in an attempted-murder case:)

THE COURT: Point that gun the other way. I only have one court reporter.

Not a Game

Q. For the court reporter, you have to let me finish the question.

A. I'm sorry.

Q. It's not like "Jeopardy" where you have to hit the button as soon as you know the answer.

The Great Interrupter

Q. Let me caution you right now that we are talking over each other, and I'm stringing my questions out—

A. OK.

Q. —and you're interrupting me occasionally—

A. Oh, excuse me.

Q. —so try to wait—

A. OK.

Q. —until I'm done.

A. OK. Sure.

Q. Then hop right in with your answer.

A Lesson in Anatomy

THE COURT: In front of me is Carol Martin. She's the court reporter. She will be taking down everything that is said. It's important that you all remember to speak one at a time so she can do that. She has two ears, but they are connected to the same brain.

Wheel of Fortune

THE COURT: The only thing I would ask you is if you would spell propoxyphene napsylate.

THE WITNESS: Napsylate, that's a variety of propoxyphene which is a longer-acting analgesic.

THE COURT: I know that. I'm not asking what it is, just to spell it for the record so that my reporter would have it.

THE WITNESS: I'm sorry.

THE COURT: In the event the People seek to make some review and it has to be provided, I would want my reporter to be able to do anything certainly more than just buy a vowel.

THE WITNESS: I would be estimating if I was to try to spell that word.

Going Crazy

Q. Let me finish each question before you respond, because if you're talking and I'm talking—

A. We're going to drive this lady crazy.

MR. KNODEL: We already have.

Explanations

Q. Now, as you obviously noticed, there is a court stenographer taking down everything that we say. She can't take down more voices than one at a time.

Even if you know what the rest of my question is or know what I'm getting at, for her sake, because she'll probably kick me under the table — she said she would before you got here — let me finish my question before you give your answer.

Does Uh-huh Mean Yes?

A. Uh-huh—

MR. GIDEON: Say "yes."

A. —unless I'm wrong.

MR. GIDEON: Say "yes." You have to answer "yes" so she can get "yes."

THE WITNESS: Well, I'm not too sure.

Licensed to Kill

Q. One favor. We tend to both know what each other is going to say. But try to—

A. You're reading my mind.

Q. Right. And you're reading mine. But let me finish my question. The same I'll try with you. Because the poor court reporter can't take us both down at the same time.

A. Is she a licensed agent?

A. She is licensed all right. She is licensed to kill if we keep doing this.

Trifecta

Q. How about the name Trident Construction?

A. Trident, Trident, Trident, Trident.

Q. Just on Trident.

A. I'm thinking of the name.

Q. Everything that you say the court reporter takes down.

A. I'm sorry, I'm sorry, I'm sorry.

Q. They get paid by the word.

A. Good, good, good.

A Friendly Witness

Q. You never changed a valve—

A. (Witness shakes head.)

Q. —in the melt shop?

A. (Witness shakes head.)

Q. You have to say something for the reporter.

A. Oh, hi.

DEFENSE COUNSEL: No, you have to say yes or no.

PLAINTIFF'S COUNSEL: Witness is indicating no, shaking his head no.

DEFENSE COUNSEL: Followed by "Hi."

Protecting His Own Head

Q. Didn't you tell me a little while ago that what you would have to do to determine the baseline is look at the exact records that were—

A. While I was involved in the care of the patient.

Q. If you and I start talking over one another, she hits one of us in the head with that steno machine, and I hope it's not me.

As in "The Little Piggie"

A. He was still in the examining room when I went to put the wee bag on the child.

THE COURT REPORTER: What kind of bag?

THE WITNESS: The wee, w-e-e. It's a bag to collect urine on a young child. He was—

MR. JONES: I apologize for the court reporter. He sometimes has difficulty with technical terms.

Scapegoat

A. I was so relieved and happy that he said he didn't feel I had cancer that I was probably euphoric and don't remember much of anything else.

Q. Did you say "euphoric"?

A. Euphoric. U-p-o-r—

Q. Well, close. This isn't a test. You don't have to worry about stuff like that. We'll let the court reporter misspell it, and then we'll all blame her.

Waving the Red Cape

Q. Let me just say that I'm having some difficulty understanding you because you're speaking so quickly. And my sympathies to the court reporter.

A. She's doing a great job.

Q. I hope she is. I see her nostrils flaring and the whites of her eyes. I hope this is getting down somehow.

Practical Lawyer

MR. LAWS: Mrs. Jones, you will have an opportunity to read and sign your deposition later on if you wish to do so. Do you want to do that?

DEPONENT: I don't guess so. I couldn't read that stuff anyhow (indicating reporter's notebook).

Contributors

Thank you to all the court reporters who sent in their funny, shocking and sometimes disturbing transcript excerpts.

Abernathy-Seal, Mary
Ackerman, Sandy
Aldrich, Elizabeth
Algorri, Karen
Ament, Kurt M.
Anfinson, JoAnne
Asmann, Lon
Atkinson, Deanna
Atkinson, Robert
Austin, Jerry
Bachli, J.
Bailey, Thomas F
Bailey, Thomas G.
Ballman, Jan
Barnini, Lisa
Batchelor, Lynda
Bausch, Susan J.
Bayalis, Sarah
Bearden, Ed
Becker, Paula
Bell, Beatrice

Benenati, Teresa
Bennett, Donna
Beora, Susan
Bergendahl, David
Bernstein, Gary S.
Berzon, Abner D.
Bjorklund, Debbie
Bleichman, Debbie
Boenau, Jack A.
Boldan, Sharon
Bolton, Barbara
Bonfilio, Jennifer
Boniface, William
Boyd, Dee Anne
Bozof, Cathy
Breech, Linda M.
Brewer, Laura P.
Brodie, Kathie
Brooks, Deborah
Brooks, Lynn
Bumpus, Richard M.

Cade, Valine
Caldwell, Lynette
Callies, Kim
Caranna, Henrietta
Carlson, Barbara J.
Carson, Jane A.
Carter, Vicki K.
Cassity, Kathleen J.
Castle, Caroline R.
Casterline, Therese J.
Casto, Nita
Caswell, Michael
Cericola, Alexander
Cero, Dawn
Chadwich, Sandra J.
Chalem, Karyn H.
Cherry, David R.
Cimms, Margerite
Citron, Corrine J.
Claar, Suzanne M.
Clark, Robert H.
Clark-Schopfer, Janice
Clingan, Andy
Coblentz, Carol W.
Cochran, Reatha M.
Cohen, Irma S.
Collier, Linda

Collins, Kathryn R.
Collins, Laurie
Combs, Merlin
Connelly, Diane G.
Cook, Ron
Cook, Sue V.
Cortopassi, Kathy A.
Crangle, Karen A.
Crews, William A.
D'Alessandro, Janine A.
Dains, Rebecca
Dalton, Darlene
Damman, Leslie Jean
Darrow, Cheryl L.
Davis, Rita
de Sevre Jacquet, Diane
DeCrescenzo, James
DeLacy, Katherine
Dennis, H.E. (Jack)
Diamond, Lorraine
Doolittle, Margie L.
Doucette, Denise L.
Drew, Diane
Dunn, Julie
Durnham, Wendell
Edwards, Mike
Emmel, Kathleen L.

Ender, Jenny
Fallon, Jeannette M.
Ferren, Janine A.
Finlay, Kim
Fiore, Kelly C.
Fitzpatrick, Frances J.
Fleet, Patti
Fleming, Richelle R.
Flores, Joe A.
Fort, Tommy L.
Foster, Florence
Fox, Matty Jo
Fraga, Christine
Frank, Jacqueline
Franklin, Carol
Freeman, Wendy
Friedman, Randi C.
Fuszner, Janet
Gales, Wesley V.
Gandy, Sally
Garcia, Tom
Geiger, Dawn E.
Gerber, Louise
Gerken, Jean Ann
Gieslinger, Suzanne
Goldsmith, R.
Gorman, Theresa A.

Goukler, Diane
Graf, Laura
Grant, Edward
Greene, Andrea
Greenspan, Rick
Griener, Margaret
Gruber, Judy L.
Gunkel, Frances
Gusseck, Sara M.
Guthmiller, Theresa M.
Haler, Sarah
Halperin, Eugene F.
Hampton, Cindy
Hansen, Linda D.
Harmetz, Vicki L.
Harmon, Margaret
Harrington, Robert E.
Harvey, Carol
Hason, Gloria
Hayine, Alanna
Heassler, Susan
Hedstrom, Cathy
Hefner, Priscilla
Hellstrom, Janis B.
Hinckley, Janet
Hobby, James L.
Hockersmith, Terri N.

Holt, David G.
Hoover, Susan C.
Hopp, Nancy J.
Horn, Tony
Howard, Victoria
Howell, Kay
Huffman, Dorothy
Hunnicutt, Jan
Jackson, Janet A.
Jamill, Juliean
Johnson, Deelana
Johnson, Doreen
Jolly, Leslie F.
Jones, Marilyn M.
Judd, Lori
Kemp, Andres
Kendy, Diane
Kennelly-Riedel, Lynn
Kikken, Debra
Kimball-Chaim, Nancy
Kimmel, Allison
Kipen, Carla P.
Klann, Patricia N.
Kocher, Roselyn
Knaub, Frederic E.
Krebsbach, Donald C.
Kriegshauser, Bo

Kruse, Carmen
Kusinitz, Carol H.
Lancaster, Marie
Landahl, Charlene G.
Lane, Jo Ann
Langhorst, Vernon
Lasseter, Lynda S.
Lathrop, Cindy
Laughbaum, Debra
Lea, Jean
Lee, Susan A.
Leonard, Wendy L.
Leone, Cherrie
Lindley, Marianne
Loomis, Bernerd
Longino, Olivene S.
Luce, Rebecaa L.
Luckett, Paula
Lyons, Patricia A.
MacKay, Laurie
Mackin, Donna M.
Mackowiak, Richard W.
Maharrey, Sandy
Mahoney, Kathleen
Malett, Rozanna
Malloy, Jody
Malone, Michelle R.

Malone, Pat
Maresko, Laura
Marks, John J.
Marlin, Anita
Martell, Joanne
Martin, Carol S.
McFadden, Lisa
McGilvray, Gail
McGrath, Dorothy
McMoran, Janice K.
McWilliams, Jayne
Meias, Julie
Menard, Linda A.
Menor, Rhonda R.
Mesias, Julie
Meyers, Deborah
Michelson, Charles W.
Middleton, Vivian
Mimma, Selah P.
Mitchell, Mary P.
Moegelin, William R.
Moell, Alic
Montalvo, Kim
Morgan, Sandra S.
Munevar, Bett
Nagy-Baker, Lisa C.
Neal, Rick

Nivinski, Lisa
Norris, Dianne F.
Nugent, Daniela
O'Connell, Catherine
O'Donnell, Joan C.
Parente, Lillian
Parkas, Tamra M.
Passero, Linda M.
Patrick, Deborah
Payne, Carol
Perryman, Wes
Pierce, Ken
Pino, Darlene
Pisano, Rose
Proper, Lynne
Purcell, Rhoda H.
Quinn, Carole
Reynolds, Gene
Rhodes-Briefer, Merle
Richards, Gene
Riley, Jeanine M.
Rimson, Rebecca
Robinson, Bett
Rogner, Ben
Rojas, Beverly A.
Royal, Russell E.
Ruesch, Antonice

Ruggiero, Deborah
Ruhnke, Eleanor
Ruthern, Lee
Sapp, Janet.
Scheid, Pamela M.
Schlenker, Dave
Schneider, Melissa A.
Schoeve, Karen
Schopfer, Janice
Schrimper, John W.
Schultz, Barbara J.
Schumer, Catherine
Seeley-Volf, Jo Ellen
Seila, Josephine L.
Seltman, Kelly D.
Severson, Jeffrey A.
Shimeta, William L.
Shipley, Beth
Shoemaker, Leon F.
Simon, Holly S.
Small, Laurie
Smith, Richard
Snyder, Joseph
Sojka, Dianna Debra
Sommerfeld, Kay
Sonntag, Gary L.
Sowinski, Laura

Spicer, Sandra
Spivak, Sandra
Stacy, Renee
Stapleton, Martha
Steiner, Dennis
Stoner, Janice
Super-Gray, Monya
Sutherland, Ian E.
Swak, Rebecca A.
Swertz, Linda
Taylor, Laura A.
Thievin, Dennis A.
Thimesch, Naola C.
Tomhave, Paul R.
Towery, Dixon
Tritchler, Carrie
Troxel, Lynn
Turboff, Alan D.
Ucelli, Susan
Waga, Woody
Waite, Marelene J.
Warren, Harold E.
Warren, Katy
Weathers, Bonnie
Weathers, J.D. (Rus)
Webster, Mary Kay
Welker, Margaret

Whately, Rhoda
White, Lawrence
Wichmann, Barbara A.
Williams, Deann K.
Wilmeth, Scott
Wolff, Mary E.
Wollin-Boyer, Karla
Wright, Martin S.
Wurm, Sue
Wuthrich, Jo
Yoder, Karen B.
Yugar, Julianne
Zimmerman, Rebecca
Zipf, Kari
Zito, Vicki
Zive, Lester
Zwanetsky, Linda